About the Author

After thirty-four years of teaching, with twenty-two years as a head across two schools, Debra Massey believes in growing lifelong learners and raising aspirations within a community. Since retirement, she has undergone a time of reflection which resonates with many:

- Who is she now?
- What options are open to her?

Through consultancy, she has supported and learned from partners, nationally and internationally, whilst leading two outstanding organisations with a focus on enriched learning and care for children from birth to eleven years. This has included a primary school, children centre and day care unique provision with an eco-focus embedded in its vision. Applying executive coaching skills interests her, shaping her 'life beyond lanyards'. Now, as well as enjoying holidays in term time and a much improved life-work balance, she hopes to support others about to take a leap into a new chapter in their lives.

Life beyond Lanyards

For Becca,

You were the most natural new teacher I ever had the opportunity to employ! Good luck with your own 'Life Beyond Lanyards' as you utilise so many skills in a new direction.

Love

Debs Massey

23.08/23.

Debra Massey

Life beyond Lanyards

Olympia Publishers
London

www.olympiapublishers.com
OLYMPIA PAPERBACK EDITION

A CIP catalogue record for this title is
available from the British Library.

ISBN: 978-1-80439-198-3

First Published in 2023

Olympia Publishers
Tallis House
2 Tallis Street
London
EC4Y 0AB

Printed in Great Britain

Dedication

For my dad, who taught me always to 'reach for the stars'.

Acknowledgements

Thank you for twelve incredible case studies who have kept me company and inspired me in equal measure during this journey.

This handbook intends to share personal experiences alongside extraordinary accounts from people who have taken the leap to start anew: the testimonials span many professions and careers and are synthesised to provide guidance for those working through this journey now – or planning future change.

Contents

Introduction

Lanyards and What They Mean

Lanyards have evolved from something you would be given at a rather nice conference, often with a laminated name and maybe even a logo, if the budget allowed. I used to collect them to ensure that, whatever colours I wore, there could, if required, be a corresponding lanyard to compliment or contrast, to blend or make a statement. *Who doesn't love an accessory?*

Nowadays, they have photos, logos, barcodes or QR access, they literally, as well as metaphorically, open doors for you in the world of work – or not if you are not trusted or senior enough to have full access across a whole site. Some may have biometric detail; some have fobs and other gadgets attached.

Indeed, it always amazed me how many small teaching resources for every new intervention my teaching assistants could attach to these lanyards... and then there were the charity-endorsed pins from Pudsey to poppies! *How on earth did they keep their posture upright with so much extra to carry, each one aiding their roles but also reaffirming their passions and interests?*

My most used was a gift from a long-standing colleague and now dear friend: it had the Robbie Williams' logo and a VIP pass which she bought for me at one of his concerts because I was unusually unable to attend that particular tour. I kept that VIP pass, even when it became damaged through age and wear until both school and day care achieved separate outstanding Ofsted accreditations (both in 2017) and then never wore any other lanyard in the workplace. It was somehow believed to be blessed with a 'superpower', my talisman: it was part of my armour, my protection. It became part of that professional mantle we all wrap ourselves in when in a place of work – and especially if that involves a role of responsibility.

So, when an established professional role ends and it isn't going to result in better responsibilities or gain increased credibility, what is the impact?

What does that mean to the individual?

What lessons have been learned?

How can a reflection on this process support others?

How can we move gladly to that world without lanyards? Indeed, can empowerment of a different kind begin to evolve?

Life Beyond Lanyards aims to explore the process and to reflect on strategies which successfully enable clear, successful leadership and the obstacles encountered. But, above all, it aims to reflect on the 'one size fits all' promise.

Hence, through social media and downright cheekiness, I have approached a variety of role models from mortal positions across a plethora of industries spanning finance, health, trade, the arts, education, and business to establish lessons learned and to share inspirational journeys of brave resilience, as each has taken that leap into the unknown. Sometimes this was enforced via ill health or a global pandemic, whilst for others, it was a deliberate and determined decision to part with the known path and try something new and uncertain.

Preface

After thirty-four years in primary education, twenty-one of which I was a head teacher, consultant head and then executive head teacher of several organisations, my exit strategy was very carefully (some might say forensically) planned.

Having decided in 2019 to leave the profession and a role I loved, when my current organisations remained recognised by external perspectives as outstanding provision, distributive leadership at all levels was incredibly strong. I planned meticulously to ensure that key staff were weaned off a reliance on me and, through appraisals and coaching, began to secure strong routes to ensure retention and further development of key personnel was subtly interwoven into training and opportunities for those who would take that mantel of excellence to a new chapter - but without me.

As part of this, what I thought was a fool proof strategy, I could become, at times, a more reflective and objective observer; noticing gaps in provision and beginning to build in more sustainable growth and opportunity: after all, the last thing either organisation needed was a resignation overload due to insecurity around changing management. Indeed, for someone often emotive in her decision-making, this was almost reptilian in its cool and measured approach. However, it also had wins for me personally and professionally too.

I began by speaking to the key inner circle of senior governors about my plans to move on in the not-too-distant future in a way that was appropriate and non-threatening. It was a philosophical discussion emerging from appraisal discussions with the expert guidance from our school improvement external adviser. All was well and I gave myself permission to seize every opportunity to be with the children and do the parts of my job I loved most, further delegating to others new responsibilities, but. most importantly, to notice and enjoy those opportunities, rather than dash onto the next diary entry at 'break-neck' speed.

One example of those treasured moments included the Remembrance Service, always involving the wider community from police to our local lord and lady, to veterans and cadets, whilst children could attend in uniforms representing St John's Ambulance or scouting organisations. As every year, we gathered outdoors to mark the silence, but somehow, in 2019, even the chilly November morning blessed us with watery sunshine and as I stood absorbing the essence of that ceremonial event, I knew my job was done at my school.

Alongside Christmas services, plays, parties and usual festivities, I enjoyed a day with our most able years five and six pupils at the Houses of Parliament alongside a wonderful team of staff who were able to sit proudly as our children debated in the roles of cabinet ministers. Again, the sun smiled down on us and a glorious stamp in my memory was forged forever. Indeed, I even applied to join the House of Lords as a cross bench peer to campaign for further support of the most vulnerable children, thinking maybe this was my destiny, only to eventually hear that I wasn't required! We laughed at school about this rare rejection, and all agreed that, perhaps, such an institution wasn't ready to move at my pace and urgency, despite my insistence.

Also, after eight years of leading day visits to school journeys, I seized the opportunity to attend what I knew would be my last school trip. It was important I didn't lead, so as not to detract from those who I was growing, but loved the opportunity to see children in a new light as they overcame fears to leap from heights and found the inner strength to overcome rain, fatigue and friendship fallouts over five exhausting yet exhilarating days. All of the week was peppered with exuberance from all pupils involved and the treasured shared laughter with so many staff who attended.

Part of my exit strategy included beginning consultancy for the Virtual School in Hertfordshire on a DFE project involving year six pupils. The focus was supporting children with a safeguarding history in their transition to secondary school. This was instigated from January 2020. As well as being a key interest of mine, it enabled one of two deputy heads, keen to explore further opportunities to lead within my school, to be acting head for one day per week.

As I have previously mentioned, I was meticulous in my preparation for leaving my organisations, aided by an extended training opportunity with the coach and mentoring through the Royal Opera House Bridge's 'Leaders for Impact' extended course. So much so that on twenty-six February 2020, after half term, I told my senior leadership team of my plans to retire in July of that year. My letter to parents and resignation to the governing board were written and all was falling into place.

Then there was COVID-19

As I closed the school *alongside all other schools in England as a directive by Her Majesty's Government*, I will never forget walking out on the playground that afternoon. The usual buzz and babble in multiple languages was muted as parents came onto the site slower and less vibrant than usual: the sky hung low with oppressive clouds and, as I walked past groups of parents talking quietly, I heard one mum crying.

Another came up to me with tears in her eyes and said she wouldn't know what to do with her four children and said a heartfelt thank you to me and my staff for all we have done within and beyond the school day: she realised she had never made her gratitude known and didn't know when she would see us again.

I continued to walk towards the older children who were being dismissed by their class teachers, Year Six charged past me, assuming this closure was just an extension to an already early Easter holiday. Little did they realise that most would never step foot in that school again: no prom, no plays, no SATs examinations and formal assessments – how could that possibly be imagined as a possibility in March 2020?

A child came up with a spray of flowers for me and said he would see me very soon, I felt my very soul contort as I realised my own tears were only just being suppressed. At that point, I caught the eye of a young male teacher who I realised saw the pain in my eyes and after the initial shock, he scooped the children away so that I could regain composure before returning to the sanctuary of my office, where I unusually closed the door.

So much for meticulous plans with forensic detail. COVID-19 was in charge now and my destiny for a life after lanyards was indefinitely on hold.

PART 1

Leaving School, Aged Fifty-Seven

Chapter 1

Making the Leap. What are the Triggers?

Sometimes reasons for retirement or a change of role are determined for us:

- Ill health
- End of contract
- Reaching a certain old
- Pregnancy
- Financial security

Other times there are subtler reasons or stimuli, interwoven with multiple strands of logic, emotional reasons – indeed, often; it's a mixture of the two.

For me, I had, what seemed to be, signposts emerging during the decision-making process, some flattering and offering exciting new opportunities for the move to 'pastures new'– *who doesn't like to be suddenly head hunted with lucrative pay awards and additional benefits, such as relocation packages, private health care?* This, alongside potential new employers who genuinely notice what you do day to day as interesting, brave, or innovative, is both intoxicating and humbling in equal measure. Imposter syndrome parked to one side for a few seconds, it can seem a very different perspective on your role and skills, especially if, like me, you have been in a particular role for some time. Albeit unintentional, it can sometimes feel that your skillset is assumed to be the norm rather than special in any way.

In contrast, the courting of a new employer versus a long-term partner has not been tried and tested, and the over-familiarity with the current position and, indeed, the lanyard embedded in that role is also secure and known well, therefore providing comfort as well as financial stability.

Therefore, despite these career dazzling opportunities and awards along the way with chances to work locally and nationally, I ignored such signposts, not because they weren't exhilarating and flattering, but because the job I had set out to do was not done, my term was not complete. For me to leave a school and day care that I loved dearly and had developed with so many incredible colleagues and volunteers, there had to be closure.

At times, this insistence to drive on, to reach a place where I could walk away knowing that the organisations no longer needed that consistency of vision was not without sacrifice and risk: especially threatening my own personal health.

My Context

Within six weeks of moving into the first purpose-built two form of entry, state-funded eco school, day care and children centre in Great Britain, incorporating family provision and education for children from birth to eleven, the expectation beyond a traditional job description was immense. After managing the early closure of the previous site due to a collapsed Tudor ceiling in July, weeks after the new build developers went bankrupt - just before the end of the summer term, with expected relocation that September, one would think that there was sufficient challenge beyond teaching and learning. However, in the first week of the September term, I learned that Ofsted, in their wisdom, had decided to inspect us. Indeed, I received the alert through my mobile whilst being interviewed by BBC TV in an incomplete carpark at the new site. (The reason for the mobile alert from our county council was because our phone lines within the building weren't quite operational!) Some of my many additional challenges included ferrying staff from the old site to the new in taxis due to the aforementioned incomplete carpark and only a quarter of the building being accessible to children and staff as multiple contractors were still completing the rest of the building. Added to this, despite recruiting approximately twenty staff to develop day care provision, unfortunately due to door handles being too low to comply with Ofsted regulations, no fee-paying childcare could cover the cost of those salaries for six weeks.

I think, on reflection, I just rolled from one issue to another without time to ask when enough was enough.

Health, however, is our right, not our privilege and through two years of working in excess of eighty hours a week and little respite in school holidays, sleep was regularly minimal and adrenaline and sheer determination can only take one so far. I ignored the pains across my chest and pins and needles in my arm and waking from dreams filled with a dread of failing. Only since then have close colleagues and governors commented on noticing me rubbing my arm in board meetings and early hours' emails during this period… *but none of them raised this, and nor did I, as, for the most part, the signs and symptoms were masked or ignored.* Many of us set unrealistic expectations of our own performance, we would not expect as reasonable for others. *Indeed, doesn't every leader at times assume the role of a superhero with powers to overcome anything, least of all their own mortal failings?* Clearly not: how simple that answer sounds, in hindsight, how arrogant, ignorant – or perhaps both, as I was at that time when the job nearly stole my right to good health.

Signpost 1

It was a Saturday October 2007 in the half term holiday and my husband was driving me to a nearby hardware store to buy paint and accessories for my office. I remember how blue the sky was and the vibrancy of the autumnal shades presented on trees, adorning our route.

Chat in the car was light-hearted and plans were being made for some day visits and family time in the blessed week ahead. Yes, I had a conference seminar to prepare for a county governors' conference, but Ofsted had gone well, staff and parents were 'buoyed up' and the children had settled into their new school building, even though we still hadn't accessed the staircase and the first floor.

It was intended that, after half term, with work prepared on the previous site during the summer term adorning every display board in the building, there would be an open evening like no other. Every child would give their families a tour around the whole site, showing where each child had artwork in a gallery to include everyone.

Rewards arising from now, growing and embedding our eco curriculum and philosophies beckoned an exciting new chapter.

I ignored the first sign: darting pain down my arm and then stiffness in my jaw.

When the pins and needles extended to my fingertips, I stopped chattering quite so much, as pain across my chest felt like I was impeded by a heavy weight.

I realised I was finding it harder to follow the conversation and when I did speak, I had to concentrate to ensure I did not slur my words.

By the time we were parking in the hardware store carpark, I felt like I was underwater, looking up as in a pool: noises seemed distant and as if from beyond the surface of that pool and consciousness. As the car stopped, I remember struggling to open the car door due to a definite weakness on my left side. I stumbled as I attempted to leave the car and lopsided reliance on a bollard adjacent to the parking bay caused my husband (now having parked the car so no longer concentrating on driving) to notice my face was slack. I could feel that I was drooling, unable to stop it. Thankfully, the professional role of experienced police officer in him took over: he bundled me into the car and drove straight to the nearby hospital.

It was only when he left me, explaining he was getting a wheelchair, that I accepted what was happening and was a later confirmed reality.

At the age of forty-three, I had what was assumed to be a TIA, a mini-stroke in layman's terms, with an outpatient referral to the stroke clinic. My children were fourteen and seventeen at that time and my plans for my beloved family had so much left undone. *That is what pervaded my thoughts in the coming days, not Ofsted nor door handles nor building projects.*

In the days that followed, I felt like I had the worst hangover ever. As days became weeks, I shared what could be hidden within half term with close family, senior colleagues and trusted governors. Most people remained unaware of this episode, but a trip to the stroke clinic and stern words from a consultant, younger than I was at that time, had enough impact to change my health and work priorities. I deliberately began to take more exercise and have realistic expectations of myself. I was driving the exponential curve of success seen by others, but the most profound advice came not from a doctor or an employer, but from my eldest son.

Tom was seventeen and took me for a coffee for which he insisted he paid for out of the wages he earned as a weekend waiter whilst at school. He reminded me how, as a family, they had agreed to support me with this new role for a year of transition to the new site, which he also pointed out with the subtlety of a teenager, had indeed become two years. With huge maturity, he explained how he understood much was out of my control and the issues beyond the new headship had escalated beyond anyone's imaginings. But he was also clear, enough was enough.

"It's like you're this helium balloon and the string is stretching and stretching so you are getting smaller and further away. But if you go completely, or you can't keep up there, Mum, they will replace you, but we wouldn't be able to."

This is what did it for me: my 'light bulb' moment of 2007. Others followed over the years, but none so memorable as this.

This signal was not ignored, I had to make changes and, actually, I had the power to do so, not only to keep myself and my family secure but to lead by example, delegate more, grow new systems and processes and to be a better role model to aspiring leaders. But above all of this, if I was to work as hard, then it had to be to play hard and live a long and fulfilling life, *otherwise what was the point in any of it?* Like the helium balloon that Tom had alluded to, the expectations of self, handed out from others, are only tangible if valued and owned by all parties, otherwise, we are trying to hold air in our hands. Juggle with bubbles.

New roles began to be developed in staffing and governance to ensure the future of my school and day care would be with sustainable leadership and that, one day, I could have a happy retirement or exit without guilt, knowing I had done my part, but that part was just a piece of the story of that place of work.

School day care and the children's centre all continued to flourish, some people moved on, others stayed and new people joined and enriched the vision of building 'my school-family.' It was therefore no longer the responsibility of one person's passions *but owned and invested in by so many individuals*. The awards and high moments swim around my head as I write, so many incredible people continuing to influence the impact on children and families today.

Signpost 2

In 2014, after multiple events filled with laughter and enrichment, successful projects and awards, came a second reminder of me being far from having that aforementioned superhero protection. Amongst many exciting moments, there were significant international opportunities for consultancy roles, ranging from the UK judge for an acclaimed teaching to a learning competition from Microsoft in Brazil. I also had two opportunities to share best practise and learn from European practise in Portugal and Germany, representing my local university, plus having a book published on leadership.

Within this backdrop, another traumatic incident came to dominate my working and non-working existence.

A little girl who had attended our nursery for seventeen half-day sessions was murdered by her father.

This remains a situation above any other that no school leader ever wants to encounter, but tragically, whenever such a story breaks in headline news, behind a devastated family are multiple professionals, all trying to fathom how on earth it could happen 'in this day and age'. Indeed, this happens more than most of us think to this day. Tragically, when it does, it can be indiscriminate and some of us touched by such a tragedy, simply never fully recover from such a loss.

Eight weeks after the news broke, whilst managing office staff suddenly dreading picking up the phone, due to press interest – albeit scripts had been drafted to refer to the county press office, photographers for national papers appearing at our school gates and class-based staff and parents remained reeling from this incident, a new norm emerged. Staff had counselling and many police interviews in equal measures and those not involved directly also seemed as if swimming in slow motion. Ironically in my last year of headship, this little girl should have been leaving primary school, if the unimaginable hadn't happened.

Again, I had pains in my arm and other symptoms building up to the previous 2007 bout of ill health, I felt terribly sick: my PA and deputy, describing me as having a grey pallor, called 101 then 999. It was, in fact, diagnosed as an 'imploded panic attack,' explained as being caused by me stifling grief, fear and distress during that eight-week period whilst supporting my school community, meaning my body was saying, 'Enough'. I was given two choices: home and rest or go to hospital to be monitored. (Since, this time, my local authority reviewed support and provision and a group of us ensured support was available for heads in the future, through face-to-face, phone calls, email advice or just a listening ear).

I accepted I was being sent home as the better of two options and my youngest son, now a trained police officer and on a day off, was called to drive me home. *In fact, on hearing I needed a lift, his first assumption was that, yet again, I had damaged our large Volvo estate car which was often badly parked and had not always been treated with tender loving care!* When he arrived, he was incredibly kind and told me he was even prepared to stay with me and watch some musical or 'rom-com' of my choosing and had announced he had even remembered that Mother's Day was that weekend so had bought bubble bath: that was when I cried. It released all that strain and distress by his self-deprecating commentary. Perhaps also the realisation that my youngest had indeed grown up and was now capable of caring for me was a stark wake-up call, as our roles were reversed.

Conversations followed with both my sons and ever-patient husband, obviously concerned about the impact of this job on my long-term health. Questions relevant to anyone taking the leap from a secure or known position to something brave and terrifying in equal measure included:

- Did I need to stay?
- Could we manage on less income?
- What support was there in the long term?
- What was my exit strategy?

Again, changes were made, but the job I had set out to do was not yet done, so I stayed, and, in fact, I am grateful for so many incredible opportunities from that point until, indeed, the time was right for me to step away. Support for future heads facing traumas or critical incidents within our local authority became more consistent, and I was one of a handful of colleagues providing outreach for those school leaders facing desperate situations, personally involved in six within the next eighteen months.

Signpost 3

Even in biblical New Testament references, a cock crows only three times and the last incident that seriously impacted my health came when least expected.

After we had successfully moved two Ofsted recognised good organisations to both outstanding grading in May and September 2017 for day care and school respectively. Meanwhile, the consultancy was raising additional income for my organisations and utilising not just my skills but that of the wider teaching and non-teaching team. Our leadership capacity had never been stronger. I had trained as an executive coach and was enjoying utilising those newly-honed skills to enhance our reflective ethos in the development of staff and governors.

At a school talent night, always a highlight of the annual calendar and consistently raising huge sums of money for the children's council's chosen charity, a mother, already known to us and other agencies for erratic aggressive behaviour believed to be fuelled by her dependence on substances beyond her own highly fuelled adrenaline, arrived, seemingly drunk, and also potentially displaying signs of drug use. Her aggressive and unreasonable behaviour, which was disruptive and intimidating at times, was subtly managed by staff as the evening settled to the children's performances. Unfortunately, it became absolutely clear this issue was not calming down and eventually out of hours social services advice was required during the evening.

Whilst I supported judges in determining the winners and runners-up, it was clear this parent could not take the children home without further consideration for their safety. Therefore, the child, who was performing, was kept back and staff ensured the parent was distracted in the main entrance whilst I finished hosting the show, intending to talk to the parent with a witness before deciding whether I could safely release the children. At that point, she ran up the stairs, only to find it blocked and began to scream at me in full view of exiting parents and children. I had her spittle on me, despite being below her on the staircase so as not to invade her personal space and, at one point, I was fearful I would be pushed downstairs.

At the time, as other heads will know, training and a securely protecting 'professional mantle' ensured I seemed fine. However, once the issue was resolved, I was visibly shaken, as were other members of staff. I was driven home as I recognised I was not safe to drive.

The next day and the day after that, I barely left my bed, feeling violated, humiliated, and uncharacteristically vulnerable. Nevertheless, I went into school on Monday but collapsed after writing my statement for the police who confirmed, as well as safeguarding concerns, that parent had committed a series of offences, including assault.

Enough was enough. My exit strategy had gone from a philosophical discussion with family to a reality.

In hindsight, what did I learn?

• There are often several signposts determining an exit strategy being necessary whilst health remains good.

• Recognising and reviewing those signposts in our working career: they are there in everyone's journey.

See the learning arising from key incidents as 'light bulb moments' for which that self-awareness enables us to make informed choices.

• I had opportunities to learn from key incidences and adapt work to accommodate those needs for me as a person, mother and wife, as well as in my professional role – and did so.

- I was bound by the expectations of others and the conventions of retirement being perceived as something you do when you are old: it need not mean this nor need it to cost you your health.

- By learning from these dramatic and challenging experiences, distributive leadership increased, and the capacity and capabilities of the wider team were enabled.

- As a role model, it is important to remember we are not superheroes and to accept something is difficult or ask for help, is, perhaps, the most surprising yet empowering strength of all.

- Think beyond the obvious in the next steps, with an open mindset.

- Seek council from people who you trust and are inclusive of you personally and professionally, including some who will challenge you with strong contrary perspectives: this approach will help you to establish what options are viable – and which are not!

Chapter 2

Best Laid Plans

The plan to retire to something part-time in July 2020, with announcements in March that year, were shared with senior leaders and chair as well as the vice chair of governors. Whilst shocked initially, in hearing that this had been my intention since the previous spring, despite multiple questions, about how the transition would happen for school and day care, they were largely reassured by the planning already in place:

• Recent training and redefining of roles and responsibilities had clarity of context which resonated with these key people in not only supporting my decision but moving forward, enabling stability for the values we had grown in our organisations so they would continue to flourish. This was largely due to a strong buy-in, especially from the senior leaders, who had been so very instrumental in shaping provision during at most, sixteen and, at the very least eight years, when we had so readily developed this double outstanding organisation. *I strongly believe we should always remember that none of us owns our place of work; we are but custodians for a time and good leadership should hand over those reins readily to a successful next chapter when that arises.*

• Development of staff, extending middle leadership capacity and with financial responsibility so that the end of multiple and creative projects was executed and with impact, as well as closure, during my remaining time in post.

• Short, medium and longer-term initiatives included a potential long lease of the adjacent community hall, a film making project with Warner Studios and Children's Parliament for the October 2021 G20 Summit. These were all secured to be potential ongoing strands for embedding the ethos I had developed but distributed to others to lead. They were keen to do so and didn't question the distribution of responsibility as this was a cornerstone of how our organisation functioned.

• Three versions of the school budget in May 2020 were presented to the governing body and separate day care budget option were also prepared, with consideration of me staying full time, part time or no longer at the setting. Yes, this was more work, but looked at three ways forward, without, at that stage, announcing my motivation being succession leadership, but planting the seed of cost and impact of options, including me:

o Continuing full-time for a year, planned in detail but costs carried forward over three- and five-year forecasts.

o Continuing full-time, but with an understanding that I would cover the costs of one day a week through revenue of consultancy, whilst extending my skill base and experience beyond headship.

o Reducing my contract to 0.8, to further develop other leaders and reduce costs on the school budget share from September 2020 or January 2021, *to gently wean me off my school and my school off me.*

Each option had carefully explained staff structures, cost savings and capacity to lead so that this seemed a healthy discussion, growing leadership from within both organisations and continuing to retain staff securely during any transition.

I have to say, I was amazed no question about my plans and impact were raised by any governors but can only think as I had been there so long, it was assumed I always would be there in some capacity.

- One day per week secondment with a department for education project based on ten to eleven-year-olds open to a social worker had already become a familiar aspect of my work, plus consultancy in other schools was the norm, as was some national and international interest. Therefore, all parties were reassured the organisations would be secure, whatever options the governors chose to examine in greater detail.

- However, COVID-19 thwarted these plans. Discussions with my senior governors, it was evident that we all assumed normality would resume from September 2020 and the governors wanted to retain me full-time from September for stability supporting us emerging from Lockdown One and returning to the school site.

Little did we know that, in January 2021, we would resume a second lockdown, but the die was cast and having deferred plans already for my exit by twelve months, I needed to ensure that, whatever COVID-19 planned next, the time had come to execute this plan.

Never have I resented nor regretted remaining in my role as executive head teacher for that additional year. Not everyone has the choices I had: ill health had already knocked on my door three times, yet to leave my beloved professional family at a time when staff and families were so very vulnerable, just wasn't an option for me. *At a time when, nationally, internationally and locally, we were all gripped by the pandemic, I knew my organisations needed consistency of not just leadership but holistic care.* For many staff and families, we were their constant through the chaos and fear, the loneliness and loss.

We moved from Lockdown One to partial opening, to Lockdown Two, to key worker and vulnerable families only having access to the site, whilst others grappled with online provision. During these periods, it became clear that the government's stipulation of a child being vulnerable if special needs were formally recognised, or a social worker allocated was woefully naïve.

More and more previously perceived strong family units showed fragility and desperation.

I will always be honoured that, when asked, the vast majority answered so openly on our return to school surveys, listing bereavements and changes in behaviours such as clear mental health implications of adults and children, not to mention the tantrums, the bedwetting, the arguments and much worse. (One family lost all four grandparents during this time: a generation of wisdom and love lost in one evil episode).

Staff phoned families at home, delivered food to doorstops, provided personalised learning – and so much more. However, especially for those without gardens (forty per cent of one particular year group lived in flats) or home shielding themselves or another family member – or for the seven pregnant staff members isolated from work, friends and family, it was an honour to support our community.

One day, I hope if teaching and non-teaching staff will be asked by future generations studying this episode in our recent experience as history to research, 'What did you do during COVID-19?' They will answer, 'I kept children learning and safe.'

Nevertheless, the next ten months are rather a blur of risk

assessments and changes of provision, often with minimal notice… no teacher is ever going to call their child after the reigning minister of education at that time, that's for sure! *I remain less than delighted, as are many, that this person is to be knighted for his professional input in politics!*

How quickly did we get used to hand sanitiser on every corner, face masks, bubbles and meetings and assemblies remotely? How rapidly did we secure a zero to one hundred per cent familiarity with and application of Google Classrooms, Microsoft Teams and virtual school trips?

The fear as COVID-19 no longer became something that was affecting someone else but we all knew someone who had tested positive. Lateral flow tests twice a week came as naturally on Wednesdays and Saturdays as brushing our teeth!

During that time, I have never been prouder of my profession and other unsung key workers, often leaving the safety of their own homes and their own families to support the wider community. The unity of clapping together on a Thursday night never failed to move me as it may have begun for the incredible NHS, *but over time, it encompassed so many other previously unsung heroes.*

Indeed, when my youngest son, a local police officer, sent me a film clip of a shift of police officers standing outside their vehicles, blue lights and sirens filling the evening air, it still brings me close to tears.

One artist and writer, Charlie Mackesy, in his graphic novel *The Boy, The Mole, The Fox and The Horse* became a daily source of hope and strength, the basis of a school plan throughout the pandemic. Quotes from his work and pen and ink images were selected by the most affected children to be emulated on a choice of coloured paper, becoming a rainbow of tattered elements in a collective place for the message of hope, goodness prevailing beyond the evil. Equally powerful and noteworthy in our entrance hall at school, this display was there as we welcomed back the whole school community, accompanied by a large fairy light-strewn tree, with hanging quotes handwritten by children during the pandemic, the positives including:

- *'I learned to dance with my mum in the kitchen.'*
- *'I taught my nan what Face Time was.'*
- *'We did board games as a family.'*
- *'I learned to bake.'*
- *'I loved walking with my family.'*
- *'We all noticed nature more.'*

Nevertheless, as we moved from September 2020 to late autumn that year, it remained incredible to imagine Christmas would be cancelled and that, in January 2021, a further lockdown would begin, plunging many into a time of despair.

So many have reflected directly to me in my work or personally, that January to 8th March 2021 was the hardest time of all. The weather was bleak, daylight hours were shortened, and hope had been snatched.

Furloughs (of which we, during COVID-19, instigated twenty-three across the school, extended services and day care, all having jobs secure afterwards, unlike so many others across the UK) meant a time of year renowned for mental health spikes outside of a pandemic, became dangerously high. *Likewise, domestic violence and child protection concerns escalated, to some tragic consequences only now, in 2022, coming into the public domain.*

It was against this backdrop that I realised despite my letter of resignation written, guidance for governors on the process and next steps drafted as requested, a letter for parents to read to their children and preparation on how to tell staff, I chose not to inform anyone beyond the senior governors and local authority until all families were back on site.

The letter was sent via email communication at 4 p.m. so that parents could inform their children and staff were protected from an immediate reaction – including me.

On 12th March 2021, the news broke, ironically the same date as the child previously mentioned and my signpost two was murdered in our community in 2014. She would have been in year six.

Once this was public, there was no turning back but beyond writing a journal during this process, there had been no capacity to plan the next steps for me.

In hindsight, what did I learn?

There had been plans for the next steps, some of them were followed through and straightforward, others a meandering path and some... definite dead ends. However, useful tools and processes included:

• Talking through plans for the long term up until announcing retirement with a coach. Finding someone who could be a mentor and ally, but not without challenge.

• For me, someone who did not work in my environment was refreshing and made me consider potentially transferrable skills.

• Keeping my decision closed to a select group of immediate family and certain senior professionals gave me flexibility on timescales and the decision of when to take 'the leap'.

• The dead ends and meandering path weren't wasting time, but determining limits of what I did want next and what I wanted to avoid.

- Life beyond lanyards took time to happen and to adjust: I needed to learn patience to establish what that meant for me as a 'quick-fix' to answer the immediate questions from others isn't necessarily healthy nor wise.

Chapter 3

Life Jacket on Self, before Helping Others

Paul Simon wrote a song explaining there are, '50 Ways to Leave your Lover.' Well, that may be the case, I couldn't possibly admit to having the worldly experience to have a view on this!

However, my school, from the moment I saw the plans for the new build, dug the first piece of soil in a JCB on the new site, I realised 'she' (*yes, always female, perhaps because I had two sons already)* was my child and I loved her dearly. Fiercely protective of her, like many a mother before me, I watched her grow and then recognised when she was ready to continue without me.

Perhaps also, having been in organisations where leaders have just 'disappeared', gone off sick or sent a message or, worse still, getting governors or other bodies to publicise a statement, this was something I thought deeply about, wanting it to be sensitive and personal, yet remaining professional and planned it accordingly.

Succession leadership is an essential and healthy strategy to include in any staff restructure or development planning and I wanted to get this right. *For other people in different professions, with various circumstances to influence how they take that leap, I have utter respect for their decisions and the reasons behind them: one size most certainly does not fit all.*

However, for me, especially having come through most of

the COVID-19 pandemic together, it felt necessary to speak directly to staff and write carefully to parents, governors, and the wider community. *That didn't, by default, mean it was easy.* Yet it was dignified, reassuring to those remaining and provided opportunities for individuals to absorb what was to be a big change, considering also, *'What does this mean for me?'*

I told staff face to face in groups and was available for individual questions and individual conversations, as were my senior leaders, who had been privy to this time of change for a year. It meant that there was confidence and reassurance about the process of next steps and reassurance for all parties – especially as we were still managing pandemic restrictions, mental wellbeing for all stakeholders was already a priority in our two organisations.

Interestingly, I could mostly predict who was shocked, anxious, and upset *and those who didn't seem too bothered*. What I didn't anticipate was the layered 'onion effect' of people gradually coming to terms with change after sixteen years of the same personality running my organisation. Due to the pandemic and picking up staff and school or day care needs, I had little time to prepare anything significant for after I left: the priority was to ensure stability remained.

One thing was very clear: I had to ensure a clean break between my organisations and me in the early days of new leadership in place, *for everyone's sanity*. Therefore, what I did do prior to announcing my departure included:

• Booking a holiday in term time from the start of September, which was refreshingly affordable compared to prior August breaks away – and cheaper still as few people wanted to risk travel due to heightened fears of getting back, thanks to COVID-19 ever-changing restrictions.

- 'Radio silence' was established by me on all social media and direct calls to anyone from my previous workplace, which was retained with the exception where bereavements were encountered. But even then, a WhatsApp message, rather than a phone call gave both parties a chance to decide if voice-to-voice conversations were welcome.

- Taking 'time out' during the process, by utilising long acquired time off in lieu which had laid dormant due to the pandemic and gave me space to think, reflect on the last part of this journey – *and indeed grieve. (I have no doubt it was valued by those staying behind too, in having regular opportunities to plan for the future, openly expressing thoughts and expectations, without fearing a comment or action could cause offence or upset to me).*

- Giving a deadline of four p.m. on 31st August when I would sign off as expectations in those last weeks, became increasingly unreasonable and stressful at times.

- Reviewing pension and lifestyle needs and wants. Luckily, we had family grown up and had diligently paid off a mortgage, but with careful management of income and expectations, I had choices and could still plan exciting adventures to look forward to. These included theatre trips once a month or a meal out – and selling a number of designer work outfits on eBay motivated that pot of pennies to be sure!

- In reviewing financial options, I chose to invest the maximum lump sum, but make it accessible if a house move, car replacement or some such major expenditure was suddenly necessary.

- A larger sum than my monthly income was left in my current account as a cushion, *to ease me into the reality that, certainly for three months, life beyond lanyards meant 'pension but life without salary.'*

- I finally adapted the spare bedroom at home into an office.

Yes, perhaps twenty-one years too late for headship, but a space I enjoy writing for various online platforms, in journals and more in-depth projects. It is a place for embarking in virtual meetings, administrative tasks, online shopping, designing Christmas wreaths and any other pursuits, meaning I can shut the door and think, plan, create.

• Likewise, it was in my newly acquired study that I tenderly put away cards, letters (which I couldn't bring myself to read until the end of August), photos of my past career and enjoy the artwork of children and others around me, which make me sometimes just look up, remember and smile. *Equally important, I can choose also to not go in there and not use the space because my time is my own and I am finally the mistress of my own destiny.*

I genuinely believed leaving my profession that I had nothing in place, but in writing this chapter, I realise much had been done to establish a foothold in this next journey ahead of me. However, some actions needed time, after this momentous change, to put in place what would gradually evolve into a new and happy lifestyle.

Learning from the value of hindsight is a marvellous thing:

• When meeting up with ex-colleagues, whilst school and day care may have entered the conversation, it wasn't focal: life beyond lanyards needs practise and affirmation!

I started considering voluntary roles which encompassed my interests and utilised my skills. This was great in principle, but, if anything, for a fear of loneliness or boredom or being surplus to anyone's requirements. As a result, I found I over-allocated time to causes and then had to narrow down some to do well, rather than spread myself so thinly that I was doing full-time hours. *Otherwise, what did I retire for?*

• Consultancy was something I considered but on reflection

during September and October, I realised to offer to support parts of leadership in schools I no longer missed (and never really liked if truth be told) was not the right way forward: the promise I had made myself was that, so long as I could live on my pension, any consultancy would be something that needed my heart and mind to believe it to be both useful and interesting. *That was incredibly liberating!*

- In my previous experience, I had undertaken consultant head teacher responsibilities for other organisations beyond my own. I knew what I charged in this capacity to bring extra revenue for my school, depending on:

o Was it a 'one-off' event?

o Were travel and other expenses included or claimed separately and if so, was there clarity of limits of charges to be bought forward?

o How long after invoicing would the organisation be expected to pay the invoice – and through what format?

o Was it for a national or international company, as opposed to my local authority or a neighbouring school?

o Was it full days or parts of days?

o Could it be undertaken in working hours and days – or did it demand holiday or weekend preparation?

o Was it for someone for whom I had worked or knew prior to the arrangement?

o Was it for more than two, less than four sessions? (This was typical of some of the executive coaching I had offered previously).

o Was it for more than ten days of contracted work?

o For longer-term projects, when would there be opportunities for all parties to review arrangements, including contractual arrangements?

o Could I offer time and expertise for free or at a significantly lower fee for feedback and testimonials, to market further client engagement?

This motivated me to sort daily rates and establish a sliding scale for the number of hours and days, depending on the time allocated to a client's needs.

• I kept the same mobile telephone number I had used from school and took over the phone contract, meaning ex-colleagues and contacts nationally still could contact me and I them. This was important on many levels, not least, as it transpired many required references for new opportunities and sought me out for this purpose.

• I set up a limited company with a logo and name through cheap and free resources online, thanks to the advice of another dear friend.

• Insurances and copyright for my work soon followed, as advised by my son, despite, at that time, this handbook and further ideas being embryonic.

• I began to gradually tap into LinkedIn more: commenting on posts of interest, but also occasionally creating posts of my own.

• I found one long-term, immediate voluntary role to support community and enrichment in learning. This gave me a sense of purpose moving forward.

• I also offered help to a local primary school. On meeting the head, I was quick to reaffirm that I didn't want a job – *and certainly didn't want her job* – I also didn't want to be a governor but hoped that still meant I could be useful. I hope to provide some coaching for leaders within that school this year, free of charge but keeping those professional skills alive and well. A truly symbiotic opportunity.

• I have since gained a flexible, part-time contract supporting those who oversee provision for children in care. By default, they are therefore the most vulnerable of vulnerable children. As my mum was in care and adopted by her deputy head, in what I remain convinced was the original 'Miss Honey and Matilda' story before Roald Dahl's legendary publication, this is a perfect role to utilise skills, my company – *and it is paid!*

• Finally, by realising what a rollercoaster this transition had been for me and recognising through social media and direct conversations how many different approaches to taking the leap towards life without lanyards, I decided to investigate strategies with human stories more closely.

• I accepted offers of interest from a LinkedIn post and another from Twitter: the aim was to begin a discussion, which if that helped one person, then I felt it would be worthwhile. I began to approach people I knew who had undertaken brave and significant changes in working roles and asked for them to contribute to this handbook to help that process.

After the time away in the autumn term, there was time to catch up, with a fresh outlook, often accompanied by cake, coffee and lunch. That too, whilst sounding perhaps shallow at first glance, gave me time to articulate where and how I was and this, in turn, enabled it to become my new normal.

Therefore, in reviewing learning to date, I realise by helping those organisations in a voluntary capacity, I was putting a life jacket on me first, *albeit obliquely*. By offering help without the fear of financial ruin in the first instance, and with realistic expectations of self and others, I breathed oxygen into my own emotional 'vital organs' gradually learning to inhale, exhale, survive and enjoy life, but with a new rhythm.

And guess what? I wasn't the only one to embark of a life

beyond lanyards. Twelve incredible professionals, all known to me and having completed some homework set by me, now have an opportunity to share the wisdom of their own experience. I wasn't alone and some inspirational people were prepared to share their journeys with signposts along the way.

A recollection of the interview process comes back as relevant to where I am in my personal journey towards life beyond lanyards.

When congratulated on the many skills I had demonstrated during the application process and interview day, I was asked by a very astute adviser from the local authority, what my most important skill to understand more deeply might be. Renowned for my complete inability to read a map under any circumstances, and realising this was an integral part of the eco-based curriculum bespoke to the school's sustainable vision, I responded immediately, 'Geography!'

The adviser uncrossed his legs and looked up from his notes, before fixing me with a barely tolerant look, before saying, 'I was thinking more on the lines of patience, Mrs Massey.'

Well, sixteen years later and I would say that skill is not yet embedded, but it is emerging!

In December 2021, my journal read: '*Happy Christmas one and all and here's to an interesting and fulfilling New Year!*'

Chapter 4

Frightened of Falling? What Happens If You Fly?

It has been four months to the day since I became officially retired from teaching and have a completely different perspective on the process of embarking on this new chapter in my life *and a new chapter in this book too!*

Most importantly, I have given myself time to grieve the loss of daily contact with those with a shared sense of purpose, bonded ever more closely by our shared experience of keeping a school and day care open throughout the COVID-19 pandemic. Those deeply entrenched relationships, some evolving quietly and unnoticed over the decade or more we had worked alongside one another, ultimately became more than colleagues, but, unwittingly, friends. Gone too is the adrenaline rush of leading a large organisation with over eighty employees with rapid and creative change management as the norm. I thought I would miss this, but honestly find I don't as the long-term wins outweigh the highs.

In stark contrast, to accept a quiet day and welcome, rather than fear, the sound of silence and my own company, has been something that was not always easy. However, whilst rushing into retirement and cramming it with busy days without time to reflect, simply defers the grieving process – and hinders useful reflection. Whilst I have, therefore, from the outset, embraced the holidays, lunches, theatre trips and coffees *without now feeling I am playing truant,* those quieter days I dreaded are now equally valued *but took more time to embrace as part of my new norm.*

I am not promising a life beyond lanyards provides the traveller with eternal youth, but now the frenetic lifestyle, without constant adrenaline-fuelled decision making and extensive work hours are no more, *I look and feel so much better*! I take time to notice smaller wins for not just me, but for others too.

I recall Socrates warning, 'Beware the barrenness of a busy life.' I really understand that now.

Once I announced my retirement publicly:

• Some extra weight which I had been battling to lose, went, slowly and healthily, and has stayed off.

• I have more time for exercise, cooking and enjoying my local area. Chores that were crammed into spare moments – or an over-reliance on my semi-retired husband are now more equally shared – *and, yes, enjoyed.*

• I can choose dependent upon weather, availability or friends or just on a whim what I can do with parts of my week, without military precision, prior planning.

• Sleep is not interrupted by anxiety about what that next day would bring. Yet anyone who knows me would never have thought the impact of my working life had such side effects. *After all, why would they, when I didn't notice it myself?*

• How lovely to visit galleries, the cinema or plan a treat visit to a theatre in the middle of the traditional 'working week' – more cheaply and with fewer crowds!

Who knew within three months, my day would always start with when I *naturally* woke up, rather than due to some synthetic bleating of a phone alarm? *In fact, the only time I ever set my alarm now is if I need to get up to go on holiday!* However, that hasn't meant I lie in bed all day or even sleep later. Bedtime and the start of my day have changed no more than an hour, *but the quality of sleep – and proper rest – are significantly different.*

What has helped me consolidate thinking and been useful to reflect upon progress and obstacles during this journey has been through writing a journal. This approach has been used by me on the direction of tutors and assessors, in long extended courses for reflection and new learning, most notably effective in my training as an executive coach but has been equally useful during the planning and final stages of retirement.

Sometimes this included lucid writing which spanned over pages in italic handwriting, immaculately recorded, but on other occasions it was questions or thought bubbles, light bulbs (my visual cue for an idea which might scatter across a page). On other occasions, a flow chart, mind map or cartoon would emerge, sometimes never revisited, but on other occasions, returned to and developed, with no pressure either way.

For me, this was not just cathartic during the transition process, but certainly reading back over the log of the last two years and recent four months, it is clear how much I had put into place in preparation for my life beyond lanyards and not all of it was probably realised at the time.

Writing a journal with ideas which have become my new reality, others that are no longer of interest and others that currently seem overly ambitious all helped consolidate that sense of where I am and who I am beyond a lanyard which, for many, determined me as an entity for so long.

Mentoring and Coaching

Despite my long-term commitment to mentoring and

coaching, I have long accepted my own reluctance to share beyond the obvious information with another, using such tools. So why is that?

• Possibly because, often, post-graduate courses came with coaching stipulations and, therefore, in my mind set, it felt artificial and if necessary, as part of the accreditation process, could I pass or fail? (I am sure this says as much about the coaches as it does of my discomfort in unburdening myself over coffee with someone I neither know nor trust?)

• Later, when training to be an executive coach, this was often alongside fellow head teachers I didn't know particularly well and really didn't trust sufficiently to admit any doubt or personal weakness in case they might judge me in some way.

Therefore, I avoided coaching for myself and, indeed, actively avoided counselling, despite seeing the positive and dramatic impact on others both professionally and personally. This was despite the very real strain of leadership on me personally and professionally, including a parent assault and child murder. Possibly this was due to being fearful of dredging some things I have taken decades to 'tidy away neatly' and move on from.

Now, I can reflect that this wasn't as might first appear to be due to a closed mind set, but the timing and the place were not conducive to that approach. *Moreover, as well as the coaching session, time to prepare and time to reflect and act upon what had come to pass simply wasn't an option: I was running at everything and now recognise the need for consolidation is not a luxury, but a necessity before taking that leap.*

In preparing for a life beyond lanyards, however, it has been invaluable and was ably facilitated by a most recent professional development opportunity via the Royal Opera House Bridge: I gained hugely from both coaching and mentor input. These two people were instrumental in me preparing for this transition open-mindedly and with purpose rather than shying away from difficult aspects of my decision. Most pertinently, four months ago and, if I am honest, even two months after retirement, was the impact on others due to my decision to take the leap. However, time has done its job, maintaining relationships where both parties recognise work was not our only shared interest or common ground, but these are maintained in spite of being colleagues, not because of this.

The final 'hooray' came after going out for lunch with a fellow head I have known for probably twenty years. We laughed, drank cocktails and barely talked about school as our relationship has evolved as our own sons have grown from children to adults and the friendship even includes stories of her three-legged dog and my beagles! The gift later received from her and fellow heads I used to enjoy time with quoted Kean's 'Somewhere only we know' and referred to Brighton conferences. To include the words of one of my favourite songs, presented in a style which coordinates with my own study and refers to time spent from 'Brighton's Best.' None of this is about a particular piece of research, neither lecture nor Ofsted inspection. What it is about is shared growth, knowledge and trust through moments where we have celebrated and commiserated over that often-lonely role of headship but often through meals out, shopping, karaoke and trips away by choice.

Perhaps, also, I have stopped cramming my diary with lunch after lunch as a reason to get up, get out and get on with life, in a replication of previous busying heightened activity, just to fill my day and reassure myself I was not likely to be lonely. That may sound rather self-indulgent, but for someone who is a Myers Briggs' 'Protagonist', communication, the stimulus of people and the pace of work life all were pretty intoxicating on the best of my days leading schools.

Yet, gradually, I have come to realise to be in my own company, to not set an alarm and not have to, in the words of Rudyard Kipling's poem *If*, then being me is enough:

'If you can dream—and not make dreams your master; If you can think—and not make thoughts your aim;

If you can meet with triumph and disaster

And treat those two impostors just the same...'

In this well-known poem, Kipling reminds us that, at times, dreams and aspirations are essential to plan and move forward but need tempering with equal doses of common sense and realism. Failure may follow success, yet from that learning process, we begin again, but from a stronger starting point. We may need to stoop down and rebuild from fresh beginnings, but if the essence of what we do is from a good place, then that is enough.

To me, this is how I worked and led but hearing so soon after leaving how some ideals were misinterpreted or ignored was hard in the short term, *but not relevant now*. It has genuinely surprised me that I have distanced myself so quickly from the organisation I grew. It was, at the time, another of my children and whilst I had expected the organisation to move on rapidly in my absence, I am surprised, as are those closest to me, how readily I have let it go. That is not to say I don't care for those I worked with nor the future reputation but reaffirms more than I knew at the time; the time was right.

Friendships I thought to be life-long simply faded due to a lack of common ground and yet, others remained stronger by the distance from the workplace and enriched by differences as well as shared interests and priorities.

Give yourself time to adapt time to reflect, time to redefine who you are: this is time well spent.

I have also learned not to take on new initiatives simply because I am asked to do so. I am interested in seeing the local museum beneath our police station become complete and accessible to local children. In my small way to have been there at its start and now as we discuss the formal launch, it has been great to incorporate ex-colleagues to inform educational provision in this initiative. Likewise, I am curious how a future exciting resource for local schools may ensure a heightened pride in where the children from my previous school live and the significant worldwide history of that place being significant from Tudor times to the present day.

I have enjoyed beginning consultancy with virtual schools, making an impact on securing support and funding for some children in care with special needs. It has been great to feel part of a new team, undertake training and... not have to be in charge!

Likewise, to accept some days will be quiet and not panic at that prospect but enjoy the ebb and flow of those days alongside the chances for lunch and visiting friends and family midweek also needs to be relished.

Life is less frenetic in cramming in busy days and more disciplined about different roles both paid and voluntary. Simply not downloading work emails onto my phone stops the habitual checking unless scheduled to work. Days out and social engagements do not get condensed by constantly cramming in work-related administrative tasks and when I do settle to work, time is managed smartly and more effectively.

Finally, I have faced failure *and realised no one died*! Having barely had experience of not successfully applying for roles with responsibilities, I have applied for a director of school improvement for a multi academy trust and a CEO for a very large and growing multi academy trust, I came second for both. What did I realise?

- My written applications are strong, even when the role exceeds prior experience.
- I don't like psychometric tests and needed to practise these with multiple YouTube tutorials to stand a chance in completing these previously unfamiliar HR assessment tools, especially at speed and being filmed for added stress!
- Presentation skills are a strength.
- I don't want to return to the stress and pressure of being in charge of large budgets or teams.
- Travel for leisure is a joy, travel for work is fine from time to time but a daily complex commute does not make my heart sing.
- Finally, both of these applications were submitted because someone I like and respect professionally believed I could do the role: flattering maybe, but during each scenario the encouragement from elsewhere stopped me listening to my own inner voice saying this wasn't right for me. I still have a tendency to aim to please others, but no longer to the detriment of my newly found independence to choose what I will and won't do. *A slow learner perhaps, as this change of mindset has only taken fifty-eight years!*

Most importantly, my pension pays for my life as it is. Therefore, there is no need to do additional roles just for the fulfilment of having a new lanyard – or because I was flattered to be asked, to be short-listed and for people I respect to believe I could do a good job.

Ironically, I end this chapter having just collected a new lanyard for my virtual school's consultancy role and I await a second for police volunteering. So, as the title of this book suggests, life beyond lanyards means we can choose how we identify ourselves and others rather than not having titles or roles at all.

What is retained, what is cast aside, in the journey towards life without lanyards?
Embrace your new normal and the differences from your past roles and responsibilities.

When attending an international education conference hosted by Microsoft in Brazil in 2008, what was clear was the importance of twenty-first century skills. Most importantly, these were:

- Communication
- Problem solving
- Creative thinking

Microsoft had little idea what was going to be needed by future generations and could only begin to predict the needs of consumers five years into the future. What they did predict was that very soon:

- Buttons on devices such as phones would be replaced with a pincer movement that would soon be emulated by toddlers accessing information: true.
- Doorbells would have cameras and remote access: again true.
- Accepting our children and further generations will have multiple careers and work as well as live longer, with pensions squeezed ever tighter and the cost-of-living soaring. Isn't it ever

more essential we aspire to be happy and fulfilled in the roles we adopt? Surely, this may well be balanced with financial gain and job security, but there are other key aspects of role relating to fulfilment, family needs and mental health that are likely to become ever more important in our workforce and society as a whole.

Perhaps most importantly, I am suddenly aware that a lightbulb is lit, and an understanding is crystallised. *Whether a new lanyard replaced the one left behind, or life is fulfilled through a broader remit, lanyards held onto too long and restrict, could become nooses rather than enabling access to new horizons.* It is from this experience that the prompts for discussion have been shared with some incredible role models who have had dramatic transitions determined by faith, relocation, COVID-19 or simply a chance to follow a dream.

Flying, not falling, is certainly what I am experiencing; some days are with turbulence, others freeing and invigorating, but to fly is to have choices both professionally and personally. This is reinforced in the testimonials of those who have also contributed to this book, for whom I am not just grateful for their insights but am humbled by their shared and varying experiences which I hope will inspire others to make 'that leap.'

What further learning facilitated me through a smoother transition?

• Look at pensions and savings to establish the best time to leap with as much security versus health and job satisfaction as a three-pronged priority.

• We spoke to our children and put our house in trust, to protect it from longer-term risk.

- Wills were updated and simplified to keep assets in the blood line, with expressions of wishes for tokens for other people or charities.

- Saying no to opportunities offered is tough but becomes easier. Initially, the fear of nothing to do can mean, as it did in my case, overloading commitments to things not of necessity nor interest.

- Multiple voluntary roles: choose something to support interests and passions rather than spread yourself too thinly and have no free time.

- Remember why you left your previous role, avoid the 'frying pan to fire' analogy.

- What are your non-negotiables? Stick to these.

- Life work balance isn't about roles, it's about fulfilment by choice. I was lucky, I had researched my pension and knew I could manage. Nevertheless, this kept a buffer in my current account, not encroached on to this day, but there to ensure independence long owned was maintained if required.

- I set up a business account, initially for phone bills and furnishing a place to work with a loan from a personal account which would be paid when viable to do so. (For me, it will be in the summer holidays in part payments when virtual school consultancy, not happening as term time only and avoids spanning a new tax bracket).

- For me a paid-off mortgage from commutation or savings - or gradually over time has provided additional freedom now.

These are personal suggestions, but practicality may determine long-term goals. Hence, Part two explores other leapers from multi disciplines for readers to cherry-pick relevant to their own situations.

If international, huge organisations cannot predict the future in finite detail, then those of us exploring a life beyond lanyards need to also recognise that some secure predictions may be possible and may become the new normal, but part of the reason for embarking on such an adventure is to embrace an opportunity for change and greet surprises along the way (good and bad) with an open mind. Flying will happen, but there may be some dips in the journey. That doesn't mean failure but ensures opportunities to customise the flight path and enjoy the opportunities to soar towards new adventures.

The old saying, 'You can't take it with you' is so true. I feel blessed to have good health and whilst never wealthy, can enjoy a golden period where, for the first time in my adult life, I can make some choices. This is not without compromise, nor is it without impact on others.

Therefore, this journey continues to be tentative but with a quietly growing assertion that this period of the present is, indeed, to use another meaning of that word: a gift. It may last a short while; it may have longevity.

Whatever lies ahead, I remain confident that I will not look back and regret making that leap – *and learning to fly, not fall.*

PART 2

Is There Anyone Out There?

A call to arms from fellow travellers on this journey.

Chapter 5

Introduction to Part Two – Questions to Stimulate Discussion and Context of Research: Introducing a Merry Band of Leapers Who Have Found Their Wings

It was crucial that the case studies celebrated came from different industries and working backgrounds, with a variety of triggers, obstacles, and learning to share as they 'flew to new heights' in a chosen brave diversion from what destiny had set about for them.

I was keen to give not a data-led summary based on statistics as the sample was small but specific and rich. Instead, a qualitative approach was preferred from the outset, reflections aiming to be shared individually and synthesised into a summative guide for anyone embarking on this journey.

The priority was to hear the voice of each contributor and to travel a short while with them in understanding the motivations and inhibiting factors along the way of their unique and inspiring journeys.

All these people were known to me, around me, sometimes crossing my path professionally. However, only when considering the richness of their shared expertise did I approach them to contribute to this handbook. Their honesty and depth of consideration were humbling and insightful in equal measure and I have no doubt they will inspire other readers as they have me.

Twelve case studies introduced to span careers in the arts, health, business, technology, finance, trade, religion and education: a 'top twelve' pick of flyers and leapers!

I really do hope what evolved will be of use to others who plan to undergo changes in careers in the future or transition to a new 'work-life balance normal' currently.

The following questions were simply prompts to:

- Gather some key information with consistency of approach,
- To gain some of each case study's own experience in their own words
- Inform others of choices and strategies successfully applied by others and to collate some 'words of wisdom' from lessons learned by those who have indeed taken that 'leap to a new normal.'

I clarified:

- I would share any draft with the case study prior to publication and they had the right to be named fully, in part, or anonymously, which was included as each case study deemed to be appropriate.
- At the point of initial contact, whether these accounts would be included as a stand-alone case study or if their journey would be included alongside that of others was not clear, but any link to them would be shared prior to publication.
- Anonymous, pseudonym or first name references were at the choice of each case study.

The following key prompts were to enable extended or brief responses, as appropriate to each case study's own situation. *Therefore, they were encouraged to extend or reduce responses as they felt was appropriate to each person's personal journey.*

The initial prompts were as follows:

• Can you please outline your role and/or responsibility before your dramatic change of work/ life decision – *and also what you do now?*

• Including any triggers personally or professionally, what made this thought crystallise and then become a reality?

• Please clarify if this was COVID-19 influenced and specifically how (due to impact on industry, shielding, furlough or other circumstances).

• Did you have any doubts or worries before or during making this leap?

• How did you feel undergoing this time of change?
  o Initially as plans began to form
  o Announcing your decision to fellow professional
  o Explaining plans to family and friends.

• How supportive were others? Who specifically in terms of advice or providing a sounding board or listening ear (if happy to share) – and how was this beneficial?

• Were there any organisations, resources or training which proved useful in supporting your change of work life?

• What obstacles did you encounter, if any, *and how did you overcome these?*

• What new positive opportunities arose which were unexpected?

• Did you learn any new skills? *If so which, from where and how were these acquired?*

• Which of your skills from previous work to new roles proved to be transferrable?

• Were there lessons along the way that you feel would be helpful to share with others?

• How has life changed for you for the better in terms of

well-being/ financial or other impacts? *Please only share at a level you feel comfortable with.*

- Is there any aspect of your previous career/ role you miss? If so, how are you managing to fill any possible voids?
- What can you do more of now that was not possible or limited in your previous role?
- Is there anything you know now that you wish you knew when you first made this change to working life?
- Any final advice for those embarking on a career change or working regime?
- Thank you for your honesty and candour in sharing these thoughts. *If there are any questions you think I should have also included, please do note them below alongside anything else that comes to mind.*

My heartfelt thanks to each of them.

Chapter 6

From Plumber to Priest: Darren

What do you get if you take a working-class lad in the 1970s from the Herts/Essex borders and buy him a pub lunch in 2022? Then add the knowledge his family were from a building trade background and he learned to talk as if he came from the heart of the East End of London when new towns emerged in the Lea Valley, changing the dynamic and culture of this part of England for always?

He was a boy who was happy with his lot and met his 'wife to be' in his local primary school reception class at the age of four. She went on to work in the city of London in the stock exchange, having gone to a 'posher secondary school' and with aspirations of her own. Meanwhile, he (as he expected) left school with a few qualifications at sixteen and, through family contacts, became an apprentice plumber.

What do you get? A priest committed to fairness, decency and his faith. Happy to welcome families back, generation after generation, for their sad farewells to loved ones as well as weddings, to new family additions and those pledging life-long partnerships to one another.

A story so compelling, it undermines stereotypical expectations of class, education and background and reminds us all what pastoral leaders and central figures in a community should all be about.

This witty, easy to talk to man is accessible to all, including all generations, and many local ethnic minorities, such as traveller families, know they will be respected as individuals. All are wrapped in his belief that everyone is equal in the sight of God. His intellect would never be overlooked again, his emotional intelligence and commitment not just daily, but notably through the COVID-19 pandemic is something from which we can all learn.

Darren brings a heart-warming and, at times, self-deprecating story to inspire and encourage us all to reflect on the impact on what we do, as he reveals how his values system was upturned and reset on a new path: from 'plumber to priest.'

'Previously I was a plumber, who had had a link through my family with attending church at a very young age. My bright red hair and a wiry build propelled by a bundle of energy were notably what I was known for. Most memorably, apparently, I was regularly seen hurtling about my local place of worship between the pews – with a liveliness and short concentration I think can probably be recognised today!

'However, as is a common story, during my teens, I stopped attending church. Meanwhile, my family continued to be involved in the local Christian community where I grew up. I now know wider family members continued to include me in their prayers, but my parents didn't create a big issue about my waning involvement in Christianity. After all, teenage interests and typical friendships took most of my time out of school. Faith versus fishing and girls were no competition in those days! Besides, my nan lived next door to the River Lea so fishing was literally on our doorstep and school mates were aplenty. Life was good, secure and happy, but in no way could anyone assume the path ahead of me.

'Leaving school with enough in terms of qualifications to prove I wasn't incapable of studying, but not enough to raise my profile beyond the typical self-fulfilling prophecy of many, adulthood beckoned, and I needed a job.

'Some family conversations were had, and I ended up working with my uncle in his plumbing business, where I enjoyed the work. The interest in sorting and fixing things and a sense of achievement for resolving a problem, or making some new system work, was something I enjoyed greatly. Also, the camaraderie of colleagues meant there was always a joke and good-natured banter, plus people who were prepared to generously and at times patiently share their knowledge with this young lad.

'I met my first sweetheart, now my wife, at the young age of four in my first days in 'big school.' At the age of eleven, however, we parted as we were destined to attend different secondary schools. We later became engaged and enjoyed great holidays, fantastic cars and a lifestyle including a honeymoon and wedding in St Lucia.

'Our focus was all about lifestyle; work hard, play hard. I remember I struggled to open a bank account as no one believed I had a salary of £30,000 a year at the age of nineteen. I suppose we were what they called 'DINKIES' in the 1980s (Double Income, No Kids Yet), with lots of disposable income and the world was ours.

'We moved out of our respective family homes together when I was aged twenty, both earning good salaries and by the time I was twenty-one, we had moved from our first flat to a three-bedroom house. Once married, life continued to be good and at that point, we decided we didn't want children: we were really happy with what we had, my wife was working in stock market and I was developing expertise in my chosen trade, both still *living close to our families.*

'Memories and highlights of that time include: three foreign holidays a year and any car I wanted. Property ownership was also a family expectation as in my dad's family with building trade backgrounds, everyone bought property. We didn't know our neighbours as that wasn't a priority: we didn't actually care – then.

'One bit of advice still rings true and long before 'Location, Location, Location' television-based advice: "Buckingham Palace in Brimsdown will only ever get you £50,000!"

'However, all of our assumed wealth was in the bank. Nowadays, my perception of wealth is rather different: "Where your wealth is, there your heart will be also," as Jesus said.

We worked hard and played hard, determined to enjoy a fulfilled life and the world was our oyster if we set our mind to it.'

Darren recalls his life-changing moment and the significance for him and his family:

'We had a great life: a nice home, close to extended family, enjoying luxuries. We decided we didn't want a family as were completely happy with our lifestyle and each other. My wife was a professional in the city, I was enjoying developing my skills in a trade I continued to learn, with job security and our future mapped out.

'Then one night I had a dream.

'I was being chased through the streets of 1920s to 30s America (like in an Al Capone gangster movie) by a group of youths when a white 1930s-styled Cadillac pulled up and

someone within the car said, "Take my hand and get in." Those chasing me stopped and said they hadn't realised I was with 'Him' and that was that. After hearing the voice from the car, I did as directed and knelt before Him. When I awoke, it was with an immense sense of well-being. This experience to me was no dream of a gangster movie, but the true GOD, the Father was reminding me of his presence. When I woke up my wife, still recalling this powerful moment, I explained that I felt I had some kind of vision: I was absolutely certain God was calling me back. More powerfully, God was calling me to do his work. We talked at length and went to church the next morning.

'As for my wife, she supported my life-changing decision without reservation. We started a family and when the children were little, financially she had no need to work but returned to a childhood aspiration of training to be a teacher. She started training the year before I started studying to be a priest. I remember us both sharing a study to work in and the rota on the wall outlining who was on call for the children's needs and when.'

Darren recalls reactions were varied from different people who knew him:

'Work colleagues initially teased me and found plenty of reasons to use my choice of vocation for good-hearted banter. I was nicknamed 'Jesus' and alerted to a number of emergencies and out of hours call outs including floods. When I queried this, the answer was pretty simple, really: "Aren't you the only one of us who can walk on water?" It certainly kept me grounded!

'Yes, there was banter and initial teasing, largely in groups, but later, the questions began to come, making me surer that my calling had a wider reach than the stereotypical expectations for

this role. When this male-dominated group found themselves dealing with a bereavement or the ill health of parents, they would seek guidance and reassurance, but they would never admit this in a group session. Masking was pretty common for men dealing with emotional turmoil, I suppose – and can be to this day.

'When we look at current statistics for men's mental health or male suicides, there is an increasing understanding of the need to support and enable accessible communication, without losing face. It was weird in a way, as it sometimes felt some didn't know what to say, almost embarrassed or maybe even fearful of my new ideals... perhaps concerned, "Will I catch it?"

'But gradually, often in one-to-one conversations that I experienced, they began asking mire questions and realised they were curious but respected my choice. Some even explored their own faith during this time.

'When explaining plans to our family, it was funny how they were fine. I had two aunties who were staunch Christians and one cousin who had started the path to priesthood after an Oxford/ Cambridge University career but didn't complete the journey. Perhaps because of this, I was advised that maybe I was better suited to being a youth worker. It's interesting to think that inherent prejudice was there, in thinking how someone like me could have a calling to priesthood. I was, after all, a rough lad, blue-collar worker, with no university or even sixth form experience surely priesthood was the most recognised middle-class 'white collar' role of all!

'Dad's family of builders were really proud from the start. I remember Dad saying to clients, "We can bury them as well now!"

When I got work at St Alban's Cathedral, wow, that was

prestigious. Family members were all so proud as there were at that time five hundred priests in Diocese, only three including me at the cathedral. I just thought it was a nice place to work!'

Learning from others and believing in capabilities, Darren reflects:

'Most of what I learned in the early days of training was from people doing things badly. It made me think about what other options or actions were possible. I have a short concentration span and am easily bored. I am known to 'get the hump' with that "can't – do" attitude. I tend to ask myself, what is the problem and how can it be solved? That solution-focussed approach draws on my plumbing background in sorting something that needed to be fixed or improved. Likewise, I believe that a sixteenth century church, such as my current parish building of over four hundred and fifty years, needs to evolve, changing to adapt to current community needs. A church is a gathering of people, not a building.

'As a plumber, my work had a quality assurance, and I wasn't threatened by the challenge or difficulty of a project. I dealt with my new role in much the same way. That doesn't mean to say change isn't messy: a few eggs need breaking to make omelettes!

'What I know now, but didn't then, is that eighty per cent of priests are introverts, likewise this trait is high for church leaders. But running an extended team with one hundred and fifty lay people, relationship building is essential: anyone can walk away at any time!'

Some obstacles Darren encountered were very down to earth:
'My salary went from £100-150,000 to £26,000 as a priest.

Over ten years, the salary increases by £1,500 difference. In fact, when my wife saw my first pay cheque, she assumed it was for a week, not a month!

'But richness is more than the bank account!

'Previously, I remember spending £40,000 on a car which I decided I didn't like after a few weeks so chopped it in for a new one!

'Being a plumber was a lot fewer hours: I sometimes miss the freedom of finishing work and coming home and the rest of the day being mine and for family. The working day ended distinctly and work was finished until the next day. As with many vocational leading roles, this isn't the case as a parish priest.

'I hadn't been to university and had little knowledge as to how I might train to be a priest, but I did it. I even found, in the assessment process, a dyslexia diagnosis which was completely unknown to me and needed some additional time and support in completing the training for my new-found career.

'I completed loads of tests and was aware that priesthood didn't have plumbers as a rule. But I discovered I had an IQ of one hundred and forty, which the bishop said was twenty points above his score! I didn't expect that of myself, and others didn't expect it of me either. Perhaps that is a very typical assumption of a lesser academic unconscious bias. I do admit to sounding a bit 'posher' when I joined the cathedral of St Albans, my wife gave me a good talking to.

'I completed my curacy in two years not the typical four, reminding myself I had this calling because of my differences and life experiences.'

Other obstacles Darren encountered came from questions of self-doubt, typical of anyone starting something brave and new:

- *'Any vocational calling is powerful and sharing concerns with my wife carried me through times when I doubted my ability to succeed.*
- *I would never have said I was previously spiritual.*
- *I asked myself many questions: Am I good enough; am I bipolar; am I really called to this? You make yourself very vulnerable: twelve to fourteen thousand people scare you.*
- *When watching Ukrainian men on news reports who have stayed, I realise it is not because they necessarily want to be, there but, then and there, that is where they are called to be.*
- *Life is scary and I would be arrogant if thought this wasn't the case and I was going to get it easy.'*

Positive opportunities arose which were unexpected include:
- Being there for people's most important family events and milestones:

'I always stop and look at the carved engraving of priests dating back hundreds of years, when entering our church, knowing, one day, my name will be there too. This reminds me of legacy, I don't own my parish, but am currently a custodian. One day, I will be just another name and the church will continue to be there after I am gone. I am fine with that, "Love 'em and leave 'em—and that's ok."

- Transferrable skills included:

o People skills and ease when talking to lords and ladies, from children to the elderly and everyone in between.

o Resilience.

o Determination to overcome obstacles.

o Strong work ethic.

o Knowledge and fascination with buildings supported Darren's parish priest role as so many churches are in constant need of repair.

Darren's calling was before the pandemic but COVID-19 influenced his role and life considerably.

'*My current role has been deeply impacted by the pandemic in ways I could never have predicted when I was ordained.*

'*Loss and bereavement were on a scale none of us in my generation or younger have ever encountered. I led seventy-four funerals in a three-and-a-half-month period during the first lockdown from March 2020. That equated to between seven to ten per week.*

'*Driving alone, sometimes with minimal family representation to say farewell to a loved one, was so tough. I recall four refrigerated containers at one crematorium and discussions about plans for potential pauper funerals and multiple coffins if required. In truth, we got nowhere near it, but hearing some saying COVID-19 doesn't exist, seemed unfathomable to me.*'

'*Honestly, managing my own fear of contracting it and supporting people in need was a huge issue.*

'*In care homes, the elderly patients were dying in large numbers. As they were short staffed, some used locum agency staff, who no doubt transmitted the disease from one care home to another, sometimes with harrowing statistics registering the impact of this. Provision for the sick and dying in full suits with PPE, whilst relatives were sobbing down the phone to me: I was powerless and couldn't see them to provide comfort as I would have wanted.*

'*Nevertheless, you hope, and knowing you could make a difference has had a long-term impact. Small conversations are no longer taken for granted.*

'*I remember distinctly seeing the first person come through the threshold of our church and how that felt, but also keeping my own fears hidden, as did many front-line workers in other vocational professions. You're petrified but draw on strength and, in my case, my faith to do the job. That level of strain for so long does sap you from within. At times, I felt emotionally drained.*

'*During the lockdowns, my faith gave me more time to 'just be' and reflect and pray. Prior to that, my alarm went off at five thirty a.m., before I was always charging through the day. In March 2020, I got up at the same time, but to take the dogs out. My wife and I walked together until 6.15 a.m.: an hour a day to talk and see the sun come up. During the darker months, we had a torch: a light in the darkness. This ritual continues to this day.*

'*We discovered that we were both good talkers but poor listeners, due to a need to 'off load at speed.' By noticing and acting upon this, our lives have been enriched by a new routine and changing habits. This has been an ongoing and positive outcome of this time in all our lives.* '

What lessons along the way does Darren feel would be helpful to share with others?

- *Don't be restricted by low expectations from others. A working-class lad has just as much right to wear this dog collar as anyone and that's the same for lots of professions.*
- *What you bring from your background is important and valuable.*
- *When an idea comes, explore all possibilities open to you.*
- *It's better to know it was not your path than think in later life, "What would have happened if...?"*
- *I've met so many eighty to ninety-year-olds who regret missed opportunities.*
- *Don't leave this world with a gravestone saying, "Returned unopened."*

'When my daughter was born, I knew whilst my life was important, she was my responsibility. Life became different.

'Some of the faith moments in my journey are shared by many in a full life beyond a religious focus, including the inevitable... what if I die? I have come to accept you can't over-plan because, instead, we all need to trust in that journey. My church role and vocation will, in the end, be another name on the wall: I am content with that: it makes me smile!'

'With a vocation, just as parents find with their growing children, the train will need to go to the next station, but sometimes last part, they go on their own.

'Now, not only a priest but team leader for multiple church communities, I have used my previous skills to help renovate the rectory alongside my dad. I am a proud father myself of two children and my wife and I have a life very different from our original plans but fulfilling intellectually as well as personally, professionally and, of course, spiritually.'

Chapter 7

From Sail to Sale: 'Chasing the Money': PW

PW started secondary education at a technical high school, which was a good school, but not a grammar school, despite him passing the 11 Plus examination. He readily describes himself as fairly academic, but the classic school report comment to cement each year's progress could be summarised as *'C+: Must try harder!'*

He loved football, recalls a fortunate upbringing, not wanting for anything and fondly remembers the holiday in America for six weeks with his family and trips to Cowes Week as his dad always had boats. Nevertheless, leaving secondary school with a handful of O' Levels was a time when possibilities for joining the adult world and workforce came into focus: considering technician apprenticeships seemed a sensible, realistic option.

Thereafter, the decision was made to join the Navy with an apprenticeship soon evolving to rise quickly through the non-commissioned ranks. He had passed various assessments linked to marine engineering in two and a half years and, after completing the apprenticeship, found himself as chief petty officer at the tender age of twenty-three. The advantages of the Navy seemed many, this role was a secure job, with a good salary and other benefits, as is the case within the forces, such as day-to-day decisions being pre-made regarding, food, clothing and a place to stay. As was the case for many a young person in a similar situation, he looked forward to a life of adventure with added bonuses of on shore drinks with the promise of romance and adventures around the World!

In 1982, the Falkland Island War tour of duty gave PW a lasting and markedly different perspective on what Navy life could entail. Returning home, he was already married and still young, aged twenty-two in April 1982. He and his first wife bought a house and had their first child, a little girl. He summarises this time in the Navy and the future ahead as realising they would 'never be rich, nor poor', and despite his boss encouraging him to consider a commission, PW felt that the culture at that time could have limited his options as he had neither the social contacts nor the Oxford/ Cambridge University background. He recognised the benefits of what the Navy offered in job security and a good pension, but after ten years' service life, and at the age of twenty-seven, was ready for a change. This was a gamble, but PW was young, and although he had a family to provide for, he decided it was time to do something completely different.

'I decided to chase the money: so where was the money?

'The best option, during the 1980s, was sales. However, focussing on my area of expertise marine and mechanical engineering from the Navy, the best I was offered was non-engineering sales roles, more of a sales rep selling hard hats and donkey jackets. I needed to prove myself in sales before trying to make the transition to engineering sales and learn the necessary new skills. I left the Navy in 1987 and started twelve months of general sales experience before, a year later, specialising in engineering sales. It was

tough: we had a five-month-old baby and two combined salaries of £23,000 which was reduced to one salary of £10.000 on leaving the Navy.

'My apprenticeship in the Navy was in marine and mechanical engineering. I started in a general sales role to gain experience and after a year was offered a sales engineer's role in the power electronics industry. This decision marked a complete change in the area of expertise to that of my Navy days and defined the path which my career has since taken. That change needed research and new understanding but also knowledge of how this would be a long-term industry to modify or adapt alongside new technologies. Gas turbine compressors versus electronics focussed products are like chalk and cheese. My reason for specialism beyond my immediate field of expertise was financially driven.

'As time went on, I worked for an American-based company with a lucrative and ever increasingly prestigious contribution to engineering sales. As is typical of the culture of such businesses in a fast-growing and evolving industry, every two or three years, a merger of companies would arise. Typically, this resulted in redundancies for some employees and new opportunities for others. I was fortunate as every time a merger took place, I got promoted with more responsibility and an increase in salary. This carried me through until the mid to late 1990s.

'With the millennium dawning, the world was full of new opportunities and many of us reflected upon life as it was and what it could be. In the year 2000, I attained the role of European sales director, with a fantastic bonus scheme. However, the only time it paid out in full was if you died in service or if the company was sold.

'I enjoyed the advantages of travelling socially and through

83

work, meanwhile, my home life wasn't great. Our lives had changed considerably from when we first met and we were on divergent paths, but I do recognise that my first wife supported me through the transition from the Navy to sales in civilian roles. On reflection, maybe we had just been too young to settle down, or at least for me, that may well have been the case. By now, we were the shared parents of two children and the relationship was not in a good place.

'The company sold in 2000, at which time I was enjoying a very lucrative salary and received a six-figure bonus. As a result of that scheme paying out in full, our mortgage was paid off, the marriage ended, with the appropriate settlement, investments also accommodated for children and a new future for me. Now in my early forties, this windfall allowed me to move on to another chapter of life. However, moving on meant personally starting again. I rented a room, from someone I knew at work, and, also through work, grew close to my now second wife and best friend to this day.

'I continued to work for the company I had been involved with, but this time under the new management. However, the company had further evolved as had its expectation: with responsibility across different time spans, aided by newly developing technology, the expectation was for me to be available twenty-four hours a day, seven days a week. It just wasn't healthy, realistic or sustainable.

'My responsibility was not only for sales but also for forecasting product demand and stock. This position was not aided by ineffective communication by others and outside my control, meaning wasted time and repetitive tasks in different formats for audiences became frustrating and onerous in equal measure. Frustration in the workplace, despite great money, meant there was minimal job satisfaction. I have no doubt a change of boss, with a different perspective and priorities to me, brought me to the crossroads of deciding the next steps most clearly.

'In 2005, I remarried and was now the father of a third child.

'Whilst on honeymoon, my wife and I agreed that it was time for me to move on. Being a senior manager, with over fifteen years' of continuous employment, a six-month notice period and over-performing sales figures meant that I was not just 'let go' and was able to negotiate an excellent redundancy package, which was converted to a compromise agreement.'

'Loyalty with impact over time is not to be under-estimated. Fifteen years with this company in its various guises deserved recognition and that is important advice for anyone leaving a secure and successful role for a new chapter: argue your worth.

'My wife and I discussed options and initially bought into a company as a director and shareholder within the same industry with someone who we had both worked with previously and a so-called friend who we thought we could trust. Things did not work out and after twelve months, we decided to part company with this colleague.'

'This was a life learning experience as not only did it cost us tens of thousands of pounds (cost of buying in), a lost friendship but also an eye opener on running your own business. We then decided to start our own business.

'Working for yourself, with the experience I had up to that moment, could not have been more different.

'In 2006, we started from scratch with no customers, no credit lines with suppliers but a wealth of knowledge, experience, *and the determination to succeed. One of my previous customers with his own business in the same industry, who had become a personal friend from the 1990s, allowed us to use his credit lines for a small management fee on the profit of every invoice. Within a short time, the initial cold calling with a lot of rejection was getting less and less, the business was growing faster than we had forecasted and we were on the up.*

'I continued to work with my good friend for a number of years until one day in 2010, as he was looking to retire, he asked the question, 'Do you want to buy the business?' (He had always agreed to offer me first refusal).

'As we knew each other well, we negotiated an agreement without solicitors and my next transition began as CEO, or managing director, of my own business.

'Once we had bought the company, we quickly grew annual turn-over one million pounds to 1.6 million and increased profitability in a couple of years: this was one of the best decisions we have made.'

However, life often throws in a curve ball and life isn't just about work, as PW recalls:

'In February 2017, at a routine eye test, I was told by the optician that there was blood in the back of my eye and was referred to my GP. The day after the blood test, I was called by my GP at nine a.m., referring me to a consultant and, to be honest, I didn't actually think too much about this, just assuming it was a cautionary check. I knew a referral was going to happen and assumed I would get a notification by post.

'What in fact happened was the consultant very unexpectedly called by eleven a.m. with the advice I was to come for further tests immediately. Looking back, I still wasn't unduly

alarmed: between one thirty p.m. and five p.m., various tests were undertaken, and I went home. For the follow-up appointment I was recommended to, 'bring your wife.' Still, this didn't resonate as an issue to worry about.'

'Then I was given the Macmillan leaflet. I had cancer.

'Chemotherapy was offered with the assurance that it should be treatable and advised that the cancer may come back but the timescale was vague in terms of months, years or even decades.

'Live to work or work to live? That was the stark reality facing me and my wife. I decided to sell the business, maybe a knee-jerk reaction at the time and when asked by her what I would do, my reply was equally direct:

"I don't friggin' know!"

'The positive answer came over time. One of my largest suppliers took me to a corporate event in Spain, where I met the managing director of a rival company who knew my personal situation – but said nothing at the time.

'Three months later, out of the blue, I received a phone call, from the rival managing director, inviting my wife and I to watch the horse racing at Goodwood. As she was already committed to an event with our daughter and could not attend, I went alone. A great day was had, copious amounts of alcohol consumed and as I was 'poured into a taxi' late that evening, I invited my host and his wife back for lunch the following day along with a final comment of, "Do you want to buy the business?"

'This friend (as he has now become) and his wife arrived for lunch – but I had not told my wife that our guest's wife was a vegetarian. A gorgeous salmon lunch was enjoyed, - and I have now been forgiven by both wives, for forgetting to mention this detail! Despite this potential 'faux pas', the potential sale of the

business was discussed over lunch and within a few weeks, an agreement was reached.

Realistic lessons emerged during this process and PW reflects on priorities and learning during this time, including providing advice for others facing significant professional changes:

'To be clear, this was not a chance to ride off into sunset

and 'live the life of Riley' but it would enable us to change our 'life priorities' whilst still maintaining a comfortable lifestyle.

'We still had a mortgage, a teenage daughter, and commitments and whilst there was equity in our house beyond the mortgage, we didn't want to rely completely on that.

'Realistic expectations were essential so that we could plan the way ahead with eyes open and retain some necessary security. Symbolically, in 2018 on my birthday, we sold the business we had nurtured and grown. I was asked to stay on and oversee the transition to the new owners in a consultancy capacity.

- *'This solution was like manna from heaven. A consultancy agreement was formalised and I could stay for as long as I liked but if we felt it was not mutually beneficial, then we would re-evaluate in a couple of months.*

- *'As a transition, it was brilliant... I would have been happy to work for Tesco stacking shelves if it meant family finances were secure. A year later, I renegotiated the consultancy rates and now work on average ten to eleven days a month and have more recently begun to support succession leadership by training up and mentoring new staff.*

- *'Here I am, four years after selling the business, still doing the consultancy, still not ready for full-time retirement and content with a great work-life balance.'*

Lessons along the way PW feels would be helpful to share with others?

- *'Any initial change is a massive step, so talking to your partner or support network to ensure they are on board, as well as professional advice, are equally important. In each change of role, personal encouragement and belief from within a relationship were essential for me.*

  Being resilient and seeing light at the end of the tunnel is key: it can be lonely working alone at home in a converted chalet bungalow garage. Cold call after cold call meant the successes came but so did huge periods of rejection.

  Continuing to strive to overcome and the constant will to succeed was essential in my mind set.

  Be financially disciplined: We had savings – but we made an agreement to not touch them for as long as we could.

  Life doesn't always pan out as you expect or hope. A failed marriage still has long-term responsibilities. I knew that the two children from that marriage deserved to be protected and provided for.

  The uncertainties associated with major life changes, whether career or health, brings into sharper focus the necessity for clarity of legacy, particularly for your family.

  Ensuring your wills are reviewed and updated as your circumstances change, whatever your age, is a thought-provoking and sobering process.

  As an individual, I was happy to take the risks but was mindful of fairness and impact on my wider family security and I did not want to undermine that responsibility.'

When asked if there is anything PW now knows that he wishes

he knew when he first made this change to working life, he listed:

- *'Knowing and abiding by your own moral code will keep in sight what you want and what you will tolerate. At times, I walked away as something didn't sit right. Also, I would rather walk away and salvage a business relationship and professional reputation. Choosing what feels right is essential.*

- *I had come from a cossetted world when everything was decided and organised for you. When I left the Navy, I had to learn on my feet and from my own experience.*

- *Building your career is a constant juggling exercise. It's important to try to keep sight of all of the balls you have in the air and make sure they are the right ones. It's OK to stop and change some of the balls.*

- *I was lucky to be working during the latter part of the twentieth century. I do not believe I could be an employer today due to the ever-growing 'woke culture'!*

- *Good mentors and good bosses had a significant impact on my success throughout my career.*

In summary, the importance of a great work-life balance, the opportunities consultancy can provide later in your career and the necessity of having savings.'

Chapter 8

Vocation, Vocation, Vocation: Sara

In the summer of 2005, Sara, her husband and young daughter were embarking on a brand-new chapter in all their lives. From being based in Norfolk and, prior to that, overseas where her husband was a squadron leader in the Royal Air Force and gulf war veteran, whilst Sara had enjoyed a successful teaching career in primary and secondary specialist provision in Germany and the UK, they were relocating from Norfolk in time for their little daughter to start 'big school' in Hertfordshire. Meanwhile, her husband was retraining to join the civilian aviation industry as a pilot and Sara was looking for a job, ideally with some professional responsibility for children with special needs.

She arrived at my then village school, interested in the advertised part-time position in a successful school, however, knowing I was leaving for a new adventure in a school which was in desperate need of her skills, I welcomed her on arrival, of course, but suggested she may also like to consider a neighbouring school with exciting adventures ahead and extensive opportunities to help me shape that adventure.

Successfully appointed as our new special needs coordinator and year six teacher, the adventure began with the first week of children drawing around themselves and draping in dance posed sari-clad figurines (who could forget a hall floor covered in paint and Sara and the children frustrated with outcomes in equal measure). Likewise, she created an exciting learning environment with a silk parachute giving a Bedouin vibe as it was suspended from the ceiling of the Tudor classroom.

Behaviour across the school, especially in year six, was, at times, challenging and much was needed to ensure the children became independent learners, but parents and children, staff and governors began to notice changes for the good and were largely supportive of a creative curriculum. Some great staff, of which Sara was pivotal in the buy-in of forging our vision for future learning and development, were intrinsically key to this progress.

When we relocated to the new site, within days, despite it still being a building site, Ofsted called; we hadn't even unpacked! In telling the staff, I vividly recall Sara drawing from a famous quote from 9/11 Pennsylvania plane crew and so poignant due to her husband's military and current civil aviation responsibilities. In hearing the imminent Ofsted inspection and knowing we were so very up against all odds, she suggested I probably had a million and one things to do, so advised me to leave the teaching to the class-based teams: as I gratefully left that staffroom I heard her say to her colleagues,

'Come on, let's roll…'

Seventeen years later, that still makes me swallow hard.

It became very clear Sara was a leader but also someone passionate about inclusion. She was loyal, vocal, and determined, even when we had our challenges from a small minority resistant to change. However, her destiny demanded further learning and therefore, to retain and grow a strong member of staff, I supported her determination to train in art therapy. It was a 'win, win' as we retained inclusive skills and enabled access to new expertise, all within the package known as Sara.

When my then deputy head moved to the first headship of

her own, it was time for Sara to move on too, following her to a new school to pick up those newly acquired tools, alongside secure teaching experience to be applied to a new context. By this time, she had worked across the primary age ranges within our setting but was clearly become ever more focussed on art therapy. She explains this lucidly and best in her own words, but in summary, it resulted in the longer term of further skill development and specialism to the role she holds today.

In her honest and detailed account across three careers, there is an ever-evolving sense of self-assurance and belief in what matters which will resonate with many.

Perhaps most poignant of all is that understanding that not all transitions and destinies are successful in the short term. However, a longer-term perspective can often reaffirm the highs and that some lows were necessary as part of the building blocks to establish a longer-term personal fulfilment and professional success.

Sara reviews that journey towards her current professional responsibilities and celebrates this is now fully on her own terms:

'Prior to retraining, I was a full-time teacher in primary education. I had held positions of responsibility as I had met the threshold so had gone from being music/ arts subject leader, then special needs coordinator as well as creativity and innovation leader.

'Now I am the therapies lead in a tier four specialist service CAMHS hospital. In my context, this meant involvement in our county's targeted child and adolescent mental health services, as provided by Hertfordshire Community NHS Trust.

'I had thoroughly enjoyed my role as a special needs/inclusion coordinator and as such had studied for a post-

graduate diploma in psychology with the Open University.

'I had previously considered perhaps qualifying as an educational psychologist but felt this was too 'dry' a profession and whilst in my role as special needs coordinator for children from four to eleven years of age, I started referring pupils to the service of art therapy.

'I went on to study for a foundation certificate in art psychotherapy and a master's in art psychotherapy part-time whilst still in my role as a teacher.

'In moving schools to a new challenge in a primary school that was graded within the 'requires improvement' category following the Ofsted inspection, changes came about: some of these were welcome, but others were unplanned and less so.

'This was an incredibly stressful time with senior leaders finding it difficult to manage subsequent local authority inspections and suggested interventions at pace, demanding to bring the school in line with the listed 'good' criteria, in order to pass the next Ofsted inspection with an improved grade.

'This ever-demanding process resulted in a deterioration in my own mental health and my physical health too.

'Anxiety and depression, combined with me being diagnosed as navigating perimenopause, meant I was, at times, unable to function as I knew I was previously able to do. This culminated in finally I realised something had to give: I really needed to leave teaching completely.

'COVID-19 did not play any part in my decision-making process as this decision, and following the changes in my career, were long before the pandemic, but in dealing with young people during and as we emerge from COVID-19, there are clearly longer and deep implications for the young people my service supports.'

When recalling any doubts or worries before or during making this leap, Sara honestly recalls:

'Huge ones!

'My daughter was having difficulties of her own at school due to social relationships.

'We had had to move her from her previous school, and this had financial implications and therefore changing career pathways was especially difficult.'

However, a support network of trusted allies, both professionally and personally, meant Sara was not undertaking these huge decisions alone.

'In 2002, when I had initially thought of moving away from teaching, I was just excited about the studying aspects of everything, it was enriching my teaching practice.

'I feel, overall, all of my fellow professionals within teaching were very supportive and understanding of the process I was undertaking and as such, I felt bolstered in confidently believing that I was making the right choice. Also, as special needs coordinator, I referred pupils to a particular art psychotherapist who was an immense support in initially pointing me in the right direction to research courses. She also recommended reading materials and generally supported me in my application for the Foundation Course at Hertfordshire University.

'Meanwhile, my family was always behind me.'

Organisations, resources or training which proved useful in supporting Sara included:

- *Open University*
- *BAAT (British Association Art Therapists)*

95

- *University of Hertfordshire*
- *My school – which was my employer.*

Obstacles encountered were largely around juggling different roles in personal and professional life:

'Work versus work/life balance was tough at that time! Submitting essays and balancing home life, especially with a young child and husband, at the time working away from the UK by necessity of his role, meant home and family alongside managing work demands were always problematic.

'Ensuring all deadlines needing to be met were factored in, but also trying to be a mum, partner and friend meant time management had to be regularly reviewed. I remember vividly there were times when I would get home to find out that my daughter had spent the afternoon in the school's sick room because she had not wanted to call me at work.'

A new and positive opportunity arose which was unexpected and remains a joy to this day:

'Then Schuyler came into our lives, enriching home and work experiences for me and others! Being able to have a puppy and be able to train her to be a well-being dog, therefore bringing her to work with me to support young people continues to be so rich an additional experience on many levels. She can be a distraction and help de-escalate young people from dark and crisis-based incidents to a place which feels safe and secure: this is such a joy. She helps support staff too.'

'I have also had training in many transferrable leadership skills, including leading preparation for audits, undertaking disciplinary investigations and root cause analysis.

'Ironically this was all from the company I now work for.'

Skills from Sara's previous work to new roles which proved to be transferrable included:

- *Being able to professionally manage difficult and challenging behaviours.*
- *Excellent listening skills*
- *Giving regard to issues of confidentiality*
- *Being able to work cooperatively and collaboratively with other disciplines.*
- *Organisational skills*
- *Communication skills*
- *Time management*
- *Public speaking*
- *Negotiating skills – diplomacy!*
- *Writing reports.*

Sara's lessons to share with others are important for any huge change in working roles, whether within a structure familiar to us or a leap to something new:

- *'Don't allow yourself to get to burnout level before calling it quits!*
- *Listen to your body and allow yourself to rest when needed.'*

And now?

'For the most part, I do have weekends now, unlike when I was teaching and later when studying and doing different roles in schools!

'I don't feel I have to plan or prepare work when I should be able to relax: there is generally a healthier divide between work and life outside work these days. I go home and in general, I do

switch off, although my husband is still my sounding board and has a far greater understanding of the healthcare system than he should have!

'I am better paid now and have more confidence in my capabilities – although I still have imposter syndrome.

'I can take breaks and annual leave when I want to and not have to take holidays in the summer holidays now. This ties in with my daughter now at university so gives more flexible travel arrangements and often I am not relying on high season charges as a necessity, as was the case when we were both based in schools.

'There are people I miss from my time working in schools, but those long-term friendships have been retained. I also recognised that, at the point when I gave up teaching, I had reached burn out, so that environment, I do not miss at all.

'Besides, the dress code is more relaxed, and I don't worry about the colour of my hair any more!

'On reflection, I wish in some respects I had done more studying alongside teaching so that I had a more in-depth knowledge of mental health issues for young people.

'It is fundamental to the work teachers do and might have been able to make more interventions earlier on in teaching. (We now have so many young people in crisis after lockdown that skilling up teachers in situ would be beneficial).'

For anyone considering taking 'that leap' Sara suggests:

'Do it, the earlier the better.

'If in doubt, do research, listen to your instincts, and allow yourself to take that change.'

Chapter 9

Conservation to Preservation: Iain

I first met Iain at a Living Crafts event where I was drawn to his stall, in awe of his wildlife photographs from around the world, not least the images of tigers. In conversation, I learned he had followed this group of magnificent animals for a decade and knew family relationships and the Indian habitat of these magnificent animals as if it was his own backyard.

Amongst other stunning photographs of many rare and beautiful global species, there were also images taken closer to home: stags with the city of London skyline and water voles at a time when they were a rare sight indeed on our riverbanks, all celebrated the wildlife within our own island in its differences and underestimated diversity.

Having encouraged Iain to come to talk to the children at my school, we soon found a kindred spirit in exploring the possibility of children capturing wildlife on their doorstep. This was at a time when he only did adult photography classes, but as his charm and extensive knowledge drew children to him in droves, fascinated with the natural world and often with blurry photographs of frogs, more head teachers welcomed Iain and the rest, as they say, is history.

From class-based workshops in multiple schools, I was keen to engage our wider family, hence family dusk walks, badger watch and other events took place, even a photographic competition. Each season, each walk provided new, exciting opportunities for 'hands-on learning' which evolved into a summit of ten schools exhibiting their work in a pop-up gallery in a prestigious shopping centre, but, most importantly, coming together to discuss topical issues around eco systems and conservation.

Yes, tigers still bought gasps from children and staff alike, but more importantly, Iain's assemblies became more focused on colour, texture, contrast, and other themes which could be shown in local wildlife moments, such as a snow-topped kingfisher or a starling murmuration.

With Lottery funding and work in Hertfordshire and west England, Birmingham and elsewhere, Iain's impact was growing and resulted in sponsorship from Lottery funding.

Then came COVID-19. Self-employed and schools-based, where direct contact was key, Iain found himself facing difficult decisions, the practicality of his work over the coming months, possibly longer, and its financial implications as he considered how to retain and extend his impact on the world around him in a way that would retain his moral compass and extensive knowledge.

'From 1997 to 2020, I worked as a wildlife photographer, the last twelve years of which I founded Wildlife Wonder, a social enterprise to work within schools on photography/observational projects to engage children with the natural world. This came about because of a head teacher inviting me into her school to talk about my work. Word spread between schools and at my peak, I was working with almost ten thousand children each year.

'My new role is a director of an animal protection organisation with twenty employees.

'The first COVID-19 lockdown brought an overnight, but

temporary, end to my work with schools. I used this time to consolidate my learning and experiences over the past twelve years, to produce resources and to provide online sessions for key-worker children or those home-learning.

'But this exaggerated the key issue for me that working alone, I had to undertake every task – a huge drain on my time and energies.

'My Wildlife Wonder work to was built around being with people, and suddenly, I couldn't function due to the pandemic. While I knew this would be temporary, it was clearly going to be longer than just a couple of months.

'In late 2020, the trustees of an animal protection organisation (that I already had a working relationship with) approached me to ask if I would step in as interim director to cover a void left by two senior staff leaving.'

When asked if there were any doubts or worries before or during making this leap, Iain recalls:

'Absolutely, I had built Wildlife Wonder for twelve years, become an expert in my area and developed amazing relationships with schools to run inspirational and vital projects with children. Leaving this was never in my plans.

'Taking on the director role on an interim basis was a good fit, something I felt comfortable doing, but originally it was just for a three-to-six-month period while the permanent director was recruited.

'My wife and immediate family were my main sounding boards as they understood me and the two roles and so could offer the most constructive support. Without my wife's support, I could not have made this transition. I also had significant support from friends/colleagues connected to the new role *though, of course, their advice always had an element of persuasive 'encouragement'.*

'It was a huge dilemma for me, to give up the work I loved and had built for a decade. Something that I did a huge amount of thinking about.

'Due to the transitional nature of the change and COVID-19 lockdown, I did not initially announce my change, but when I made the decision to make the change permanent, it was one of contrasting emotions, sadness to say goodbye to my old world, but huge excitement at my new role and what I knew I could achieve in it as part of a team.

'My friends and family were hugely supportive; I think they had seen a change in me while undertaking the temporary director role.'

Pros and cons of the new role:

'The biggest obstacle was the huge amount of learning I needed to do, while also being in the deep covering the two senior leadership team roles.

'There was so much to learn! While the role I was taking on had a significantly higher level of responsibility and pressure, working with a team eased many of the burdens of self-employment and the transition was eased by the training which was provided and offered by my new employer.

'Just some skills due to change of role and leading a team, rather than working as someone who was self-employed included:

- *Application of new technology*
- *HR issues policy, development, legal parameters and public relations on a national and potentially international scale*
- *Applying a need for delegation*

'I now have the security of a regular, though modest, salary (I work for a charitable organisation) which does allow me to focus on the task at hand and not be burdened as to whether I had paid work in the next month, in three months... This is always a headache and emotional drain on self-employed people.

'What I soon realised is, for anyone embarking on a change of career, planned or otherwise, you will probably have many more transferrable skills and expertise than you imagine:

It's easy to feel in awe of the experts around you and whilst you will have much to learn, you will already have much experience and new ideas – or ways of doing things that will be of great value in your new role.

• Listen to others and ask questions, but don't be deterred from challenging current practices. Many things happen in a particular way, not because it's the best way but because that's the way it's always been done.'

Lessons learned Iain feels would be helpful to share with others:

• Ability to work with people is key.

• I enjoy being with people and my work has always been centred around successful communication. Therefore, whilst in a very different role now, these people skills have been so important.

• Successful communication is at the heart of both my new and old roles.

• Being self-employed, I understood finances and financial prudence, so these were transferrable.

• My in-depth experience in education has also been a skill that has been useful in my new role, the organisation I lead has a very active education team.'

Change isn't always without sacrifice, but comes with benefits too:

'My previous life involved much activity, time outside in nature and working directly with children. I miss all of these. My role now is mostly office based. I hope over the coming months, I can take time out to get actively involved in some of the education teams working with schools.

'I lead a team of twenty people, have professional advisors/consultants and a supporter/membership of tens of thousands. The scope and reach of what I can do are massively more than I previously could!

'However, I now have the security of a regular (albeit modest) salary, which enables me to focus fully on the tasks at hand. As a self-employed person, I was always thinking (whether at nine p.m. at night or on a typical Sunday morning) about the next invoice and work for three months ahead: this became a significant time in my working week and, at times, an emotional drain.

'As such, my stress levels have changed; whilst my new role has much more pressure, it has much clearer time boundaries and work/life balance.

'When embarking on this career change, one thing I didn't know. But do now: it was going to be a good move.'

Finally, Iain would recommend the reader to:

'Go for it! That is my final advice: but don't burn your bridges, so that if, after giving it a good go, it isn't working, you could return to your previous career!'

Chapter 10

Lights Out and Lockdown: Working through and beyond COVID-19: Tom

When need overcomes prior training and skillset, you can sit back or seize a new opportunity, just because you have to do something.

This was Tom's stark reality, during the COVID-19 pandemic.

As a highly successful musical director of international acclaim, Tom was determined to learn new skills when COVID-19 closed West End theatres overnight, to provide financial and emotional security for his family during the pandemic. There were no guarantees when this industry would resume nor how.

This father of two boys, both suddenly studying secondary curriculum through remote learning at home, needed to juggle supporting his family and saving his home. No scheme protected performers during the turbulent time ahead and months became years as, gradually, the theatre lights came on once more. What Tom was keenly aware of was a need to act quickly, parking his expertise and credibility in a tough yet rewarding industry with years of prior respect and success, to survive and come through the pandemic with what mattered most intact: his family.

I was lucky enough to know Tom initially through my role as head teacher when his children attended my school. His passion for music resulted in him launching annual talent competitions for us by ensuring the whole school participated in various improvised and set pieces. This included a version of *We Will Rock You* with volunteers with no musical experience being given the opportunity to try tuned and un-tuned percussion, electric guitars and mass body percussion, involving 380 children, all successfully enthralling and inspiring his audience of four to eleven-year-olds – and adult staff in equal measure. He also would play impromptu requests and free jazz when attending assemblies and joined our Parent Voice Committee. I have the utmost respect for this person as a professionally skilled individual, but his humanity and realism during the pandemic celebrated an inspiring change of direction, with planned and unplanned gains now likely to be long-term.

Always so encouraging to our state school in extending creative experiences, Tom was quick to share upcoming projects and whilst we watched many a show with groups of children including *Annie* with Miranda Hart playing a quirky Miss Hannigan, it was equally great to take a coachload of parents and staff to see *The Bodyguard* with Beverley Knight in the leading role. Tom was announced at the start of the show as the production's musical director, to great applause which meant he was filmed whilst still leading the orchestra for the school's Twitter followers! One of his unsung talents is his tolerance for my exuberant enthusiasm, even when untimely!

His other recent shows have included *Bat Out of Hell* and the also critically acclaimed *Hamilton*, to name but two of many highly successful productions in the West End of London. Tom's sons also performed at school, one being offered a musical scholarship at secondary school, both winning our annual talent show on drums and piano in solo performances as inspirational and different in style and content as these two young men are as people.

Tom's passion for music and live performance, coupled with an absolute commitment to his boys, meant this book would not be complete without including his recent, inspirational story:

'Until March 2020, I was a professional musician, conductor and arranger. Although I am still those things now in any spare time that I have, my working day has changed dramatically. I am now a court manager for HMCTS (Her Majesty's Courts and Tribunals Service). I came to this role by working as a logistics manager for a large retailer.

'Being forced to assess my working options over a matter of hours and days meant I had to find another way to keep a roof over my family's head in some extreme circumstances. Due to my travelling as part of my performing, I did not have peripatetic pupils or other online work which would have been able to support a young family or mortgage. I have always been interested in the law and justice, but it wasn't until I held a managerial position in a large company that I thought, "this could be for me."

'My change of direction was entirely due to COVID-19 and the immediate shut-down of my creative industry. This industry did not begin to recover until mid to late 2021, and even then, with multiple attempts at restarting, there still remains a risk involved for investors and producers, causing tours and shows to close early, or, indeed, not open at all.

'My only concern was that I needed to find work quickly. Any other thoughts about my decision came more slowly.'

When asked about the feelings experienced along the way as change was necessary rapidly and outside of prior experience at work, Tom reflected on this in three contexts:

• Initially plans began to form which he described as, '*A mix of loss and a gratitude for a new role.*'

• When announcing your decision to fellow professionals, he recalls, '*There was little discussion between my old colleagues about how we were choosing to get by.*'

In explaining plans to family and friends, Tom was aware that protective measures for others, simply did not apply to those in his industry:

'*Some family and friends were furloughed, but they all knew my industry had been wiped out overnight so were not surprised I needed to look elsewhere.*'

On reflecting on the support available, Tom was clear that personal support and a newly accessed professional infrastructure enabled confidence and belief in taking this leap, but he also recognised that he was fortunate in finding an accessible employer who encouraged and enabled the development of new skills.

'*My partner had a similar experience with her own industry and was unable to continue with her business which she had just set up. We both knew we needed to find work, whatever that may be.*

'*I was lucky to find a company that valued all staff from day one of arrival. There were opportunities to be taken and ways to progress. Attending work every single day through lockdown enabled me to meet a wide range of people, all with different reasons and circumstances that led to our meeting.*

'*The company I first joined favoured promotion from within and also provided a great range of online learning resources, from computing skills to management techniques. My role now comes with a huge range of learning and development opportunities, as well as experienced staff who are willing to mentor and lead.'*

When considering the obstacles that were encountered and how these were overcome, Tom recognises the need for planning with his partner to cover home life and that family responsibilities were key, as was a shared understanding that these changes were driven by immediate need, at least to begin with. He also noticed some unexpected opportunities too:

'I was lucky that there were very few obstacles. Shift work proved difficult with home-learning hours and children, but my partner and I shared the hours as best we could.

'Management training, additional responsibilities, first aid qualifications and new career opportunities were all new and unexpected outcomes of this change of working role.

'I realised that my experience with working with people and having had a 'managerial' role for many years meant I had transferable skills in new settings and industries.

'Almost all jobs involve working with others and how you interact with those people can have a huge effect on the quality of work you produce together. I learnt to type, improved my knowledge of good HR practice as well as writing and preparing reports and looking for solutions to problems or improvements to current processes.'

When this enforced transition from one industry to a completely different professional responsibility emerged, Tom recalls:

'I saw myself returning to full-time music work as soon as possible, but I turned down a short run three-month contract on a West End run for two reasons:

- *No guarantee of work after the contract ended. This had*

never really worried me before as I kept in contact with other industry colleagues and there had always been cover work available to fill my diary until the next job came along. The pandemic showed me how vulnerable a 'non-essential' job could be and that any recovery could be protracted.

• I was enjoying being around more and a six-day evening working week would mean missing more concerts, school events and evening meals as a family.'

When asked if there were lessons along the way, which would you feel would be helpful to share with others?

'If you approach a challenge with an open mind and a positive attitude to make the best of what you currently have, opportunities will come your way that you could not have predicted. All experience gained has value.

'My work-life balance has improved greatly, and I am still getting used to having time and space at the weekends to see family and friends. I am able to take my children to activities and enjoy watching them do things they love and have a real talent for. I have time to be around so much more and would not change that now.

'I do love performing and I am lucky enough to be able to cover playing and conducting roles on a part-time basis, around my daytime work. I have also been involved in online workshops and seminars with students looking to enter my original industry.'

To lose Tom's current new role and responsibility he now realises that:

'I would miss the people and their work ethic. I would also miss the satisfaction of knowing that I have played a small part *in improving an outcome for someone. A very different experience from performing, but no less fulfilling.*

'Nevertheless, I value most of all spending time with family and friends and make the important events in their lives.'

When asked if there is anything you know now that you wish you knew when you first made this change to working life. He replied:

'Just how far I would be able to take the opportunities in front of me. Don't let a lower wage impact on your choices – if you find something that works for you, interests you – and challenges you, go for it.'

Chapter 11

A Leap into International Opportunities: Work Hard/ Play Hard: Jane

When first encountering Jane, two things were significant: her immense capacity to throw herself highly successfully into many sports, versus her exceptional interpersonal skills. The competition and teamwork of the former trait, combined with the ability to work with, and lead teams, were equally evident at a young age and are just as relevant to her varied and highly successful career choices and changes to date.

Jane then travelled overseas, utilising a passion for skiing and entertaining to embark on roles still in her teens and early twenties as varied as skiing instructor to later attending catering college and hosting sumptuous events, always with an interesting and varied group of people both diverse in roles, outlook- and life experiences.

It is little surprise to find so many inherent traits adapted to become transferrable skills as she trained to be a nurse, constantly seeking further training and professional development in, at times, highly specialist fields, with an increased reputation for the quality of what she delivered. She worked in NHS wards and evolved through multiple management roles. As time went on, she was head hunted for further high-profile specialist projects across London hospitals and later, international consultancy, enabling brave projects for the benefit of women and children's health to result in a state-of-the-art provision.

Within what is already a packed portfolio of expertise, Jane instigated a recruitment business and has reviewed holidays and facilities overseas, incorporating her beloved tennis into the mix of 'work hard, play hard.' Sport has always been a key aspect of Jane's social life, but also essential in that balance to do something she loves outside work.

Jane, like many, worked throughout the COVID-19 pandemic, most specifically being actively involved in the strategic planning for the Queen Elizabeth Unit at the Royal London Hospital (which was a shell and had two core floors adapted to accommodate one hundred and seventy-six intensive therapy unit beds). Through this delivery of service, crisis management was required, but with assured experience and expertise in equal measure. Her intrinsic involvement in a team, aiming to roll out such critical provision for so many souls critically unwell, was essential to bolster the number of acute and intensive care beds previously available.

To this day, she remains committed to health development but has launched herself outside the of 'mothership' of the National Health Service, realising her needs, as well as those of her employers, to retain the fulfilment and drive of what she loves, but with a clear plan of an exit strategy from part-time to being fully retired.

Typical of those who love sport, her focus remains sharp on her current expectations of herself and her longer-term work goals. However, perhaps reaffirming her determination to utilise transferrable skills, Jane acknowledges networking and learning from others retains her interest and opportunities, currently and in the future.

'I have had a couple of major changes and major work

decisions in my career to date. Whilst some of these were planned and the product of training for a key role, others arrived through a more unexpected route – or evolved as one project seemed to lead to another.

'Having trained as a nurse, it was time to decide if I wanted to go into nurse management or operational management. Having chosen to do the latter and completed an MBA (Master of Business Administration), I managed an extremely large service in the NHS with over five hundred staff and the third biggest unit in the country.

'After doing this for several years, I realised that I had completed what I felt I could achieve – which, with my superb team, was a huge goal reached.'

'This, then, was my first big leap.

'I left a job I was successful at and with the security of income and infrastructure, for life to set up a business for health care recruitment (permanent positions only). This was motivated by one of many 'bug bears' I had: the NHS had so many agency staff, costing a fortune to this national institution, with people earning double what the loyal permanent staff earnt.

'On the back of this, I also set up a health care consulting company. Both companies were extremely successful for ten years when, sadly, the large recruitment companies used health as a market share rather than a money earner and crippled small businesses, so, sadly, I had to close our doors on one of the businesses, making several staff redundant. This was not an easy time, but with leading a team, comes responsibility.

'I believe having good leadership skills and communication skills helped with telling the staff and as the recruitment business was so transparent, this didn't come as a shock to most of the staff as they had had very few placements over the last year. This was a last resort and done with careful planning and preparation.

'However, the consulting business carried on and from this, I was head hunted for the second big leap of faith when I left the UK to go abroad to commission a new hospital.

'Whilst both were dramatic changes I undertook during my career; I knew that I could always be able to be employed back in healthcare if these projects did not bear fruit.

'It's not about leaving skills from training behind to try something new but building these into the planning of the next steps. Realism is necessary to ensure multiple outcomes are planned and considered before taking a high-risk change to working roles. We all have bills to pay, after all!

'Once returning to the UK after the project completion abroad, I returned to a lovely job in the NHS working part-time for service developments, working with stakeholders and users to get the best for their services. This I will do part-time until I fully retire.

'During the COVID-19 pandemic, my role changed due to the immediate need from the ever-increasing numbers of very sick people. I was drafted in to increase the intensive care beds in London: my so-called part-time job became a sixty-hour-a-week role. Whilst I can say I am now back to a normal working week, this does not translate as back to my part-time hours quite yet!'

Including any triggers personally or professionally, Jane considers what made these career changes a reality:

'I always wanted to have my own business and had a huge amount of support from family and friends. I truly believe my trigger was that I felt I could not improve the service I managed any more and I was getting frustrated, so it was time to go and *there was no other job that I wanted to go for.*

'I was also in a very lucky position that I knew I could go back if required!

'There are always nerves at the beginning, 'am I doing the right thing' is something most people would ask during such a journey. It is a huge ongoing worry, whether I was going to get any work.

'When you start employing staff for your business, that comes responsibility beyond your own financial security and that is great to support the viability and longer-term growth of the business, but not without risks. There is a wage bill at the end of each month, so the money must be there to be able to pay staff. You feel responsible for not only your mortgage but there's as well!

'For a private business, if there is no money coming in the door, you still have wage bills to pay at the end of each month, as well as corporation tax, VAT and all other overheads, IT, phones and so it goes on. Therefore, you do feel responsible to ensure there is enough money coming in to pay staff and all bills and to try and make a profit so you can expand and give pay rises and so forth.

'It is not like the public sector where the money is always miraculously there to pay the bills. As a result, it can be hugely stressful having to deal with cash flow and motivating staff to work hard.'

When asked about how did she feel undergoing this time of change, Jane reflects:

'Initially, as plans began to form, I had huge support from family, and they were included from the outset in my plans. I spoke to a few professionals from different walks of life who had

their own businesses, who encouraged me, gave advice and assisted when I needed help. It was very exciting writing a business plan for my own business and a five-year strategic plan.

'In announcing your decision to fellow professionals, I had no issues. They were all very supportive. I left a senior management position in the NHS to set up my own businesses.

In summary, I had a huge amount of support from family and other business acquaintances. Throughout my career, to engage with others is always beneficial whether for advice or just as a sounding board.'

Obstacles versus opportunities:

- *'There are always obstacles and trials and tribulations, and this is, again, where you need support from outside perspectives whom you trust to talk to.*

- *The main opportunity was setting up a consulting business which, when I decided to leave the NHS, I had only decided to set up one business. In fact, this became my longer-term initiative and continues to provide exciting working opportunities for me today.*

- *I feel you are always learning and setting up a business is the biggest skill I have ever learnt.'*

In considering the use of skills from previous work to new roles proving to be transferrable, Jane is clear:

'All leadership and management skill are transferrable but additional support most useful included:

- *Bringing in a bookkeeper monthly.*

- *Using a firm of accountants to support when required.*

- *Accessing a broker for professional and public liability insurance who assisted me in this.*

- *Luckily, I never had to use a solicitor!*

- *I had expertise in HR and recruitment from my role in the NHS and was able to call on 'friends' when required.*
- *Regarding terms and conditions, I did this all myself and used bits from other recruitment companies to make my own. There is so much you learn from the internet!*
- *Within my previous NHS senior management role, I had a huge budget, and, at that time, things weren't centralised like they are now, so I learnt good negotiation skills for purchasing. I think this helped with negotiating daily rates.*
- *I also researched a lot of how other consultants charged and had conversations with various people who advised me.'*

In reflecting on her lifestyle, both personally and professionally, since her leap into running her own business, Jane considers these key elements to have had the most impact:

- *'I would say the main one is networking and meeting so many different people along the way.*
- *As these events are all to do with my career and I am meant to be in a part time role now, I don't miss anything! I got out of senior operational management at the right time!*
- *I do have more time now to play the sport I want, still, not enough time to play golf, that will happen when I retire at sixty!'*

In considering knowledge and hindsight, Jane is clear:

- *'I should have done it earlier! And I certainly should have worked abroad earlier. The highlights in terms of working abroad were beneficial financially and culturally whilst extending my own experiences professionally and personally.*
- *It was amazing working in a different culture and having to learn extremely quickly the cultural challenges. In a realistically short period of time, I have made lifelong friends, as*

we were working so closely together to complete a very challenging target date to open the new hospital.

- *Don't be scared and follow your dream!*
- *Have faith in your thoughts and go for it.*
- *Don't regret not doing things. Life is too short.'*

Chapter 12

Back to the Classroom, with a Thirst for Learning: Florence

Florence is a bright and reflective person who has many transferrable skills. However, due to her extreme aptitude for scientific enquiry, she discovered that her highly specialised award-winning work drew her further and further away from a childhood dream of being a teacher. Successful in management and research, highly confident in leading teams and secure in a reputation for excellence in her research fields, accolades were many and rightly deserved.

So, what was it that made this professional re-evaluate her role and career in her fifties?

It is said by those who are wise, that good health is not our right but our privilege. Florence knows that all too well as she had the devastating diagnosis of breast cancer when, otherwise, she was a fit and capable professional – with the bedrock of a loving family and strong faith to enable continued growth and impact on self and others.

Typical of her character in the working role and personal relationships, when approaching her recovery, she did so mindfully of others and her own needs, thought deeply and then got in touch to ask about routes into primary teaching.

From a teaching assistant role to a now experienced and highly effective class teacher, it has been a privilege to encounter the grit and passion, in equal measure, with which Florence has fought her disease with dignity and determination. She literally started over from 'ground zero' in a career which could not have been more different from spreadsheets of complex data and insightful synthesis of that information into recommendations for further development of science, to benefit our society as a whole.

However, in her reflections on this journey, this leap of faith to fulfil a need embedded within her childhood aspirations, perhaps replacing data for children and their progress holistically and academically had more transferrable skills than she might have imagined.

I have no doubt if she were to work for the government in making schools more effective and processes more streamlined, then her impact could be far-reaching indeed.

'I was the director of systematic review at an international company, a pharmacoeconomics consultancy. Our core business was supporting the pharmaceutical industry in their submissions to regulatory authorities for reimbursement of drugs and devices. This business was well established in international status, with submissions to many boards and governments around the world.

'The systematic review team conducted and analysed data from clinical trials to assess the safety and efficacy of drugs and devices and calculate a cost-benefit ratio. These data then used by the relevant licensing authorities to agree or refuse reimbursement. This team was the largest, and the most profitable within the company. It was also one of the largest systematic review teams in Europe. I managed a team of up to twenty highly qualified analysts and writers. I was also responsible for their training and development. (More about my interest in teams later).

'We made a point of publishing our work, demonstrating its

academic rigour. Indeed, we won several medals and prizes over the years for our work at international conferences.

'In addition, I sat on the senior leadership team of the company and was a key player in business planning across the wider company.

'And now? I am now a primary school teacher in my fifth year of practice.'

In considering any triggers personally or professionally, Florence was asked what made this thought crystallise and then become a reality?

'Following breast cancer in 2011, I decided to reduce my stress levels, eat well and exercise more as these were the only things within my control that might lessen the chances of a recurrence of my cancer. This had nothing to do with COVID-19 as decisions and actions to change my career predated the pandemic.

'For me, this meant a change of career. I had wanted to be a teacher since the age of five, when I started school. Somehow, it never came to pass, as my A levels were science-based and pointed me towards a career in science. My PhD further narrowed my field of vision and I worked for many years in pharmaceutical business. Thanks to a broad business training scheme, I was lucky enough to work across several disciplines: mergers and acquisitions, business planning, marketing and sales and clinical trials. I became interested in the theory of teams and their management and worked hard to build successful teams under my management.

'I felt that I could put my communication skills to good use as a teacher. I also believe that my own curiosity and constant desire to learn would offer something to education.'

Florence, typically candidly, shares feelings before or during making this leap that were integral to the process:

'Yes, of course, I had doubts and worries.

'I worried about my age and the risks around starting again. I was fifty-two. I worried that my career would be short so would it be worth it? I worried about taking a seventy per cent pay cut and the effect that might have on my family.

'I was concerned about what teaching would actually be like, having read and seen on the news about the number of long-term sick and teachers taking early retirement. I worried about going back to university and studying with people the same age as my own children. I worried that it would be extremely hard work and take up all my free time. I worried that I might not be any good at this new role, so different from my previous professional responsibility.

'It was certainly daunting, stepping into the abyss, having been right at the top of a ladder and starting again at the bottom.'

Florence reflected upon other feelings undergoing this time of change when:

Initially, plans began to form: *'Stressed but excited and proud.'*

Announcing your decision to fellow professionals: *'Nervous but excited and proud.'*

Explaining plans to family and friends: *'Proud that I was making a change and facing a challenge despite all the worries previously outlined.*

'My family were amazing. They knew why I wanted a change and were fully supportive. We discussed the financial implications

and the fact that I would be working six-day weeks for the training period at least. I know this did make me unavailable for various social activities and did impact my husband and children. However, I was lucky that they were all behind me. I could not have done it without their support.

'My friends thought I was a bit mad but were very supportive and encouraging. They stuck with me and now, often remark on how they saw me grow and blossom!

'My neighbour, who was a successful primary head, was also supportive: giving me practical advice and support, as well as acting as a professional sounding board and listening to my trials and tribulations!

'Once I was at university, my fellow students (three in particular) became a very close bubble. We went through it all together and spent many hours sharing joys, sorrows, successes, failures and tears. They were critical support.

'Faith was important as when I stepped off the cliff, I needed to know that there was a pair of hands there to catch me if I were to fall. It definitely gave me the courage to take the leap.

'I was also lucky in that my husband's best friend had walked away from a successful career as an industrial scientist, in his late forties, to re-train as a secondary teacher. He followed the PGCE route but never looked back. Knowing someone who had already made this change definitely helped me come to my decision.'

Florence did plenty of research and decided to take on a non-teaching role to gain informative insight. The money was low, risk high but by doing so, her raised understanding of a new discipline had long-term benefits.

'I took it upon myself to get a teaching assistant job for twelve months prior to teacher training, as I wanted to go into teaching with my eyes open. It was probably the most important 'training' I did! I then had to complete a year of teacher training, so I was placed in a school and had to attend university. The academic training was provided by the university and the practical training by my placement school. I was also lucky enough to attend training courses at places like Herts for Learning.'

In terms of obstacles, Florence recalls *'Getting the first TA job was hard because I was fifty-two with no prior experience in education. I believe I was also seen as a threat by some teachers and heads because I was more qualified than they were, and I had more managerial experience. I got the third job I applied for. I was persistent, organised and learned from each interview.'*

However, new positive opportunities arose which unexpectedly included:

- *'Classroom management. It was very different from training compliant adults to unwilling children.*
- *Learning about learning difficulties and how to adapt my teaching to a differentiated audience.*
- *Safeguarding and child protection.*
- *I now have a level 1 coaching qualification from the Football Association.*
- *I intend to continue my own self-development. I am still learning.*
- *The joy of studying and teaching a broad range of subjects. I love that because I am interested in EVERYTHING!*
- *To discover a whole new academic interest in education and learning.*
- *To meet new people who are not scientists!'*

Transferrable skills were multiple and included:

- *'Teamwork*
- *Organisation*
- *Work ethic*
- *Goal focussed*
- *Wanting to be the best at what I do*
- *Accurate record keeping*
- *Professionalism*
- *Training and development*
- *Management skills*
- *Academic rigour*
- *Broad interests (subjects across the curriculum)*
- *Sense of fun*
- *I have lots of good ideas*
- *Desire to constantly improve*
- *Positive mental attitude*
- *Flexibility*
- *Playing a musical instrument*
- *General knowledge*
- *Being a good communicator*
- *Being a good role model.'*

Lessons along the way which Florence feels would be helpful to share with others?

- *'To try before you jump, if possible.*
- *Don't go in blind. (Teachers are also child protection officers, counsellors, administrators, in loco parentis, referees – and more!)*
- *Do your research.*
- *Make sure those around you are on board and share your*

vision. It will be a bumpy ride for them too.
- *Don't be afraid to dream, believe you can do it!*
- *Remember that the children have no idea what you don't know/didn't plan/ forgot to say.*
- *Have fun!'*

Florence realises that her life changed for the better in terms of well-being but financially there were losses to bear:

'Financially I am much worse off, but I have found out so much about myself. Mentally, I have never been happier. I really do LOVE my job. I can't believe how good it feels to know that I make a real difference to the children I teach. It is a huge responsibility, but such a huge buzz. I want to be an outstanding classroom teacher.'

'I am passionate about my own health and fitness and that of the children I teach. I try to be a good role model and I believe that it helps that (at school) I was completely hopeless at most sports. I believe that the children should know that it is fine to take part in sport whether you are any good or not. Not everyone will be a school runner/ county runner/ national runner for example, but that doesn't mean you can't take part and enjoy the sport anyway. Specifically, my Football Association qualification shows that I can teach football and enjoy football, even though I am not very good at it. I encourage the children to compete against themselves rather than others. Healthy eating is important too and I do have the opportunity to cover this in science and PSHE. I suppose my aim is to get the children to make wise choices, for themselves.

'However, I do miss some of my colleagues, but I do keep in touch. I miss some of the international travel/conferences. I have

to make do with reading the journals now.

'I miss the money and also, I miss 'being in charge' as I often think I could do a great job as a senior member of staff. I often look at the management/processes in schools and think it could be much better-or more efficient! However, having started at fifty-two, I am clear that my ambition is limited to being an outstanding classroom teacher.'

With what Florence knows now, what does she wish she knew when first making this change to her working life?

- *'How much paperwork there would be!*

- *How horrible parents can be, developing a thick skin is very difficult when you care passionately about your job.*

Most of all though, I value the opportunity to have fun and be silly, spending time with young children.'

Chapter 13

CEO to Self-Employed: Alan

Since leaving school in 1982, Alan has carefully, and, at times creatively, created a portfolio of business interests utilising a natural instinct and a never waning interest to keep learning and trying new challenges. Within that time, he has learnt from others, become more interested in researching successful strategies employed by others and gained a confidence built upon strong interpersonal skills and a rightly deserved respect within the financial services business community.

Alan has been hugely successful across a range of work environments, not least based enviably in London's Mayfair in investment banking, where his expertise soon escalated him to senior positions and CEO roles. He reflects when asked, *'There's always something on an internet search to teach you most things you need to run your own business and incorporate a limited company.'* This ongoing leaning has been alongside being equally successful as an independent consultant.

However, from designing catchy business names with clear logos and branding to stand out from the crowd, website design and more generic skills, Alan is typically understated in how such success has come about.

He reflects that he has 'retired' more than once but has learned, between new projects, to give himself time to choose ventures that are right for him by selecting options which have proved to be lucrative – but also interesting.

During the journey, he was often self-taught, acquiring new skills that, in large corporate environments, would be delegated to others to perform.

When discussing recent projects, he lists investments in a high carbon mine, a vineyard, cyber security software, a gold mine, marketing data software, FinTech and education overseas as just some initiatives which have sparked his imagination and harnessed his highly extensive skillset.

Alan is far more than a singularly defined professional, but what is clear is that excellent communication skills, including a genuine interest in others, alongside many transferrable skills, means that he embraces change and developments in the business world and has a keen determination to shape his working role to welcome and embrace future developments and all that may offer.

'I am an investment banker and have been CEO of multiple blue chip financial services businesses. I set up two businesses of my own just before the start of the pandemic (one in investment banking and one in corporate marketing). For me it was not a dramatic change, as I am used to running a business, the only difference is I wasn't a shareholder before and therefore, for these ventures, I needed to deploy my own capital.

'If change is a dramatic one then it is not always the right decision unless the new situation has been forced upon you by surprise, although I would still argue change at some point is inevitable for us all, therefore we should anticipate it.

'It is critical for anyone to have options in life and not to let others control your destiny at work or at home. To be in control, you need to make time to develop new skills, knowledge and interests which will help confidence and resourcefulness in the

ability to move on and maybe take on a new job. There is little point in having a plan that is not well researched in terms of business ideas or more personal lifestyle objectives. Most individuals I advise did not do enough before the change.'

In considering any triggers personally or professionally, to make 'the leap' to running his own businesses, Alan believes:

'I was motivated to change as I wanted a more flexible lifestyle as I approach retirement.

'My change was not influenced by the COVID-19 pandemic, but it has certainly been restricted in terms of developing new relationships in the new business lines that I am pursuing. This obstacle was overcome by offering to meet business partners and clients and this was largely solved by Zoom and Team video calls.

'I had no worries as such, other than winning business on my own. I am fortunate to be financially secure and confident in my own capabilities.

'Initially, as plans began to form, I felt excited and when articulating the business proposal to fellow professionals as well as family and friends, I found it easy as I had a clear vision and objective.

'I didn't get any advice from anyone, other than Google Search on things such as accounting procedures and legal advice and fine detail.

'I always read as much as I can on business and personal development. There are thousands of publications out there, – you must take the best parts and make them your own.'

Alan soon realised some new positive opportunities arose which were unexpected:

'New business lines materialised from existing contacts,

many previous work colleagues clearly rated me highly and generated unexpected work opportunities.

'I learn new skills every day like marketing techniques or web site construction. I acquired all my new skills from reading online publications and tutorials.

'Transferrable skills were very evident and relevant to the success of these new enterprises. As an experienced CEO, I was well placed to run a business on my own, I have been fortunate to acquire a lot of knowledge and skill in all business functions.'

Lessons along the way Alan feels would be helpful to share with others:

- *Be and stay focused on what you are trying to achieve.*

- *Always remember the rule of three: never have more than three objectives about what you want to achieve and what you want to communicate.*

- *Always consider a wide audience: don't over-rely on professional jargon or acronyms in your communication as often extended and specialist vocabulary doesn't communicate levels of understanding and benefits to others.*

- *Be kind to others with your time and knowledge, often what you give out, you will get back.*

- *Be smart with your time, sixty-four per cent of your results come from just four per cent of your most effective time.*

- *Get organised and develop the knowledge and experience before you make the change.*

When asked which aspects of his current role he would ring-fence as part of his preferred tasks and challenges, Alan recognises a preference for providing consulting services at this stage of his career: he does not choose to become involved in delivery-orientated tasks.

Whilst considering what he would like to further develop his business roles, he is very clear, his primary goal is always to improve my marketing skills to develop new connections.

Meanwhile, when asked to recommend any reading which Alan has found inspirational around him changing roles and growing new businesses, he suggests: 1 PAGE MARKETING PLAN: Get New Customers, Make More Money, And Stand Out from The Crowd, by DIB ALLAN.

Alan recognises that he now has a lot more allocated free time for family and friends. He enjoys additional freedom of choice around when to work and how and is happy to decide what he wants to do each day. He looks to the expected future of employment with the final advice:

'The Organisation for Economic Co-operation and Development (OECD) predicts that by 2030, fifty per cent of the working population in its member countries will be freelance workers, the pandemic has accelerated this. That is a massive shift to self-employment and dynamic working practices. I recognise that for many, this will be a challenging decade and now is the time to build new skills and habits to prepare for an inevitable change in workplace culture.'

Chapter 14

New Home, New Country, New Life: Sharon

Sharon is a force of nature! Everything she does, she commits to one hundred per cent and that is both in a personal as well as professional context. Her pace of life, whether work-related or beyond that context, is impressive, adding to her organisational skills, creative thinking and sense of humour, she collects ideas and people at speed to make changes happen for the greater good.

Her strong moral code and close family unit combine with a firmly rooted religious faith to shape decisions, and which have, in turn, determined life-changing decisions for her and her family.

Whilst happily settled in a life with affluence and professional success, with a young family and a job she enjoyed, she was recognised through the responsibility and opportunities her life in South Africa offered. Sharon nevertheless moved from the other side of the world to the United Kingdom, to start a very new and markedly different adventure, with her husband and children.

In considering triggers, barriers, and advantages of the enormous change of life for her, – and indeed her whole family, she realises that the decision once made was not one everyone around her endorsed. However, surrounding herself and her family with positive support and strong faith to guide her, this journey has bought happiness and different opportunities, for which she remains grateful.

No regrets, but a strong family unit was essential in making this experience positive and enabled the transition to a new life by being confident and positive in her approach to decision making.

'Before moving to the UK in 2007, I worked at one of the top four Banks in South Africa (Nedbank) as a specialised portfolio manager in the retail banking division where I worked closely with divisional executives and regional management. My clients were the twenty-seven thousand people employed across the country who worked in the retail banking division. My role entailed:

• Management development: providing access to gaining a business degree equivalent for identified 'highflyer' through a partnership with GIBBS Business School,

• Graduate development: visiting universities around the country and recruiting from a pool of graduates to fulfil the needs of the business, whilst giving graduates an opportunity to gain valuable work and personal experience in the workplace,

• The Letsema Learnership Programme: in partnership with the Government Blue IQ Project, matriculants (which are the equivalent to school leavers in the UK at eighteen-years-old). This initiative provided a one-year contract within the banking environment to provide essential life skills training, as well as work experience for those enrolled on the programme.

Induction programme management: Designing and maintaining the programme for all new employees in the retail division (countrywide). This included marketing material, audio-visual content, training the trainers, liaising with divisional and regional management for information and participation in the programme.

• Performance management and& recognition: Managing

and ensuring the successful implementation of the group performance management model as it related to recognition. This included:

  o *Presentation to, and facilitation of, all regional nomination committees*

  o *Ensuring all nominees met the selection criterion and had followed the nomination and selection process providing an executive summary to the retail executive management showing division, race, gender and grade breakdown.*

  o *Planning and executing regional and national functions to recognise the winners and reporting all information to the group HR team.*

I currently work at a primary school in Hatfield as an HLTA (higher-level teaching assistant) based in year six. My responsibilities include, but are not limited to:

  • *Supporting the class teacher during lessons, this could be with individual children or working with a particular group.*

  • *Classroom and corridor displays: updating working walls in the classroom and creating and maintaining the year group displays in the corridor once a unit of work has been completed.*

  • *Safeguarding of children and reporting any concerns promptly.*

  • *Lunchtime management: managing the rota for a team of fourteen people who work across lunchtime, ensuring three hundred and eighty children are fed, supervised, and that play opportunities are planned to engage them. This also involves me working alongside the Community Support Manager to interview, recruit and manage the team.'*

A dramatic change in work opportunities made this thought crystallise and then become a reality:

'The move to the UK was triggered by my husband receiving a job offer from a company in the UK. The reason we made this life-changing decision was to provide a better opportunity for our children.

'We decided as a family that I would take some time away from the corporate world whilst the children settled into life in a new country. Accepting that the transition would impact each family member differently but equally significantly, meant we were realistic in what we could do to support this and how I might best manage my time. This gave me the opportunity to help with class trips and re-kindled my childhood desire of working with children. I enrolled for a distance learning diploma to become a Teaching Assistant, secured a permanent job and within a year, I had enrolled to 'upgrade' to an HLTA (Higher Level Teaching Assistant).'

Sharon remembers clearly that there were understandable concerns whilst embarking on this leap:

'It is impossible to make life-changing decisions without having doubts or worries, but we talked it over with each other, family and friends - and we prayed.

'All our friends and family were very supportive – sad that we would be leaving, – but excited for the opportunity we had before us.

'Most of our friends were exceptionally supportive, helping us to sell or give away our furniture, helping us to pack and even looking after the house once we had left until it was finally sold. We did have one or two friends who felt that we were abandoning the country (and them) and wouldn't talk to us any more – we have since resolved these issues – but time was needed to heal and reassure all parties.

There were many times we questioned if we were making the right decision, but each time we thought there was an obstacle, it was removed and that, to us, was a sign that God had our back and that as long as we trusted His plan for us, we would be OK.

'It was nevertheless a nerve-wracking time, – there was a lot of documentation to be completed as the company in the UK had to prove they had tried to recruit locally. We also had to sell our home and most of our belongings which was very stressful. We had to look for new schools for the children – only using the information we could find online – which we found quite difficult. It was a short turn around, so we felt quite overwhelmed at times.

'Our best friends were invaluable and were an incredible source of strength and support – to the point where we had reached our limits and we called them at ten p.m. the night before the moving company were arriving and they arrived twenty minutes later with pizza and stayed with us all night helping us pack up the things we were taking with us. They were definitely our rock and anchor through the whole process.

'My mom and dad were also instrumental in our journey as they were able to provide support from the UK, getting the children enrolled at school, meeting the head teacher and helping to sort out the paperwork.

'It takes a village to raise a child, as they say – and we certainly needed one!

'I was nervous about telling my manager as I had a lot of different responsibilities, and it was right in the middle of all the selection processes. He was very supportive and together we formulated an exit strategy.

'We had involved family and friends from the onset, but once the decision was made, it still felt very surreal telling them we would be leaving the country. Emotionally, we felt everything from elation and excitement to worry and despair.'

Organisations, resources or training which proved useful to Sharon included:

- *'I had been reading a lot of leadership material, such as John Maxwell, Who Moved My Cheese? Which I found to be exceptionally useful in that it helped to change my thinking from 'I can't do it,' to 'Let's give it a go.' Everything is a learning opportunity, and I knew that if it didn't work out, I could always go back to what I was doing before.*

- *'Our faith helped us a lot.*

- *'Moving to a new country is daunting, however, our faith remains the same to this day. Finding a Church and being able to connect with others enabled us to ask questions and find out information about certain areas that we would otherwise have been oblivious to, such as where to live, how taxes work, not to mention, questions to ask at our childrens' school.'*

Obstacles encountered and overcome were around the children's education: systems and processes were so different to that experienced in South Africa:

'School systems were so different! From what is taught to how it is taught, especially content and terminology. I enrolled in some courses that were provided by the school community partnership (aimed at parents to help their children with homework). I asked questions, observed, and researched what I didn't understand.'

An unexpected and positive opportunity arose which redefined Sharon's working life:

'An opportunity to work in a school was a really life-defining moment for me. I would never have had this in South Africa as I did not complete any teacher training. With the support of the

school, I successfully completed my HLTA (Higher Level Teaching Assistant) status within six months (due to the department closing because of restructuring).

It was then I realised essential transferrable skills from my previous career to my new role:

- Managing *conflict*
- *Solution-based thinking*
- *Ability to prioritise*
- *Time management*
- *Interpersonal skills*
- *Experienced communicator*
- *Computer skills.*

In completing a diploma to become a teaching assistant and then onto complete the higher-level teaching assistant assessment status, these transferrable skills were intrinsic to my success. These courses gave insight into how to plan lessons.'

Lessons along the way Sharon feels would be helpful to share with others include:

- 'Change is always going to be scary. Research as much as you can and ask others who have taken that route to give advice rather than take advice from people who have never been in that situation before. Try to focus on the positives and that will help to overshadow the negatives.
- 'Talk to family and friends, ask for help and accept the help offered!
- 'The impact of being at home more and not travelling over four hours a day to work is unquantifiable. I am less stressed, I am more present and I feel I am able to be more effective.
- 'This reflects on the relationship with both my husband and the children as well as family and friends in general.

- 'Even though I am earning significantly less than I would be if I had stayed within the corporate field, we have learned to discern what is important and necessary rather than impressing others.'

Sharon accepts that there are some aspects of her previous life that she misses but she seeks fulfilment in other new ways.

'I do sometimes miss travelling and meeting new people, sitting around a table and brainstorming the next big project or function.

'However, I re-direct my passions to looking at different ways to improve things at school for the children and being active in our church.

'I have been able to spend more quality time with the children and my husband.

In my previous role, I did a lot of travelling (as did my husband), so we didn't have a lot of quality time together. Being able to just walk the children to school and chat about everyday things rather than just helping with their homework, has enriched all our lives.

'I understand the children better and we can relate to one another much more easily, they feel comfortable just sitting and chatting with us.

'Any regrets? I wish I had been more confident in my ability in teaching. I would have pursued a degree in teaching and spent the last ten years teaching instead of being a higher-level teaching assistant.'

Another move, another adventure beckons, meaning Sharon is currently able to reflect on lessons learned last time:

'As we prepare for our next move, although it is within the

borders of the United Kingdom, many similar challenges and opportunities present themselves as we faced when leaving South Africa.

'Drawing on our previous experiences, on what worked well and where we can learn and do things better; we have been guided by the following principles:

- *Know what we are looking for and be prepared to wait for it.*
- *Have a 'wish list'. Be specific, but also know what we are prepared to compromise on.*
- *Use the experience of those that are currently living in the area to guide on location, pricing, and other influential factors*
- *Embrace both the excitement and trepidation of what the future holds, after all, it is our experiences that add spice to our lives!*
- *Having faith to trust that God has prepared the way for us.*

Furthermore, before embarking on any decision to move, we first discussed the opportunity as a family – taking into account both pros and cons of staying where we are and moving.

In any life-changing event, it is important to have all parties on board, especially as children grow older; they want to feel that they are listened to and that their opinion matters. The upcoming move poses new challenges and opportunities, in that each of the children are in different life stages: the eldest has just finished an apprenticeship and the youngest is in the final year of university.

'Whilst looking for new jobs and a new home may seem overwhelming, thinking ahead and managing the risk does help in keeping focused on the positives and keeps the process moving

forward.

'Career changes are inevitable as life changes with marriage, children and expected, as well as unexpected, circumstances all play their part. It is paramount that knowing what you enjoy doing and being confident in the skills that you bring to the table can greatly impact the success that you have. This is the case, whatever path we choose.'

Final recommendations Sharon would like to share, for those embarking on a career change or working regime:

- *'Trust your instincts, take the plunge – whatever happens, good or bad – it's an experience. We always said we would rather look back and say, 'well we won't do that again' and not 'I wonder where we would be now if ...'*
- *Life is always going to be challenging we will only know if we can if we try – and who knows, maybe you discover you are great at it!*
- *Be careful whose advice you trust, true friends will have YOUR best interests at heart, not theirs.*

Throughout the times in my life when a leap has been required, I have found that having a positive attitude, a willingness to learn and being open to all opportunities that present themselves is a winning combination.'

Chapter 15

Engineering a Historical Legacy: Peter

Peter is a man who has a combined skillset of technical expertise and a passion for aviation history. He is a natural problem solver; someone who has applied these skills to an engineering career which, whilst being mostly self-employed, has had long-term contracts with key providers.

Whilst his learning and skills are always developing, he realises some parts of the industry are not sensitive to change and proactive in approach and do not have 'Teflon coated' assurance of continued success. He has worked with companies beyond his immediate area and retains a consultancy business for projects now and in the future, – as and when they might arise.

His love of aviation history combined with his expertise in engineering resulted in active involvement as a curator of a museum. This was both in a paid contracted capacity, as well as having previously been one of a team of volunteers.

As that door closed, another opened, in fully overhauling an old, crammed store cupboard beneath a police station which, with the support of key police personnel, he has adapted what in yesteryear was an air raid shelter, into a resource for local children. This is now packed with objects of interest, items to be handled and an exciting learning resource for primary-aged pupils.

Again, Peter demonstrates life beyond lanyards may not always be on our own terms – and certainly not always straight forward – but perhaps in the long term, the journey might, after all, be richer for that process.

'Before my retirement, I was a self-employed contractor with my own one-man company which I had used since 2001 to work on various contracts, mainly in the transportation, and also health and safety, sectors.

'My main source of work was from a specific consultancy company in which I was an equity partner. Contracts included working for a privatised part of London Underground as a project manager, rail signalling (working in the business development department for four years) and the London Heathrow terminal two on a large construction project.

'However, the consultancy, unfortunately, went out of business in 2016, leaving it difficult for me to find other work, due to the specialist nature of my specific previous role.'

An opportunity 'flew in from out of the blue' using Peter's skills and interests – and also provided a salary.

'Since 2006, I had been a volunteer at a local aircraft museum, with a powerful and important legacy of British aviation to share with generations to come. It was through this initially voluntary role that an opportunity arose for me to successfully apply for a contract to become the museum's curator. I first undertook a short-term contract to support the museum's bid for National Lottery funding for a major development project: this went well, and in early 2017, I was appointed as the curator on a twelve-month renewable fixed-term contract; I was still working through my consulting company during this time.

Once Lottery bid was successful, I oversaw the redevelopment of the museum from an interpretation/ curatorial perspective, until my contract was terminated in October 2020.

'As curator my job at that time included:

- 'Day-to-day collections management (receiving new items, loans in and out, disposals, collections and exhibit care).

- 'Giving talks outside the museum and conducting guided tours for visiting groups. This included hosting visits by school classes and youth groups (cubs/ scouts/ brownies and other community groups).

- 'Contributing to TV programmes being partly filmed at the museum for BBC, Channel 5, Yesterday and also, Discovery Channel.

- 'Dealing with specific historical and technical queries from the public, whilst also overseeing the management of the museum archive.

- 'As part of the Lottery-funded project, I was also instrumental in writing the new interpretation material for a new hangar and the redeveloped existing hangar, in collaboration with the design company engaged for this purpose. I was also heavily involved in planning and executing the movement of the museum's aircraft and other exhibits once the new buildings were ready.

- 'Through representing the museum at meetings of professional bodies such as the County Association of Museums, alongside other local and regional forums, other opportunities arose. One example involved me providing specialist support to a sponsorship contract with a Swiss luxury goods manufacturer. This also involved me attending their marketing events in the United States of America, Europe and the Middle East.

- 'During this time, I was also the line manager for two

museum employees, namely the events manager and the learning officer.'

Not all options and changes to working roles are through the luxury of choice, but Peter is pragmatic about options from both needs and reality perspectives.

'I did not make the decision to retire and had no wish to do so. After thirty-four years in the engineering profession progressing through various jobs (and moving from PAYE employee to self-employed consultant in the process), I had finally ended up in my ideal job working in the aviation heritage sector. I was working with old aeroplanes, which I loved, and was being paid to tell people about their history and technology. The money was not particularly good, but with no major financial liabilities such as a mortgage or children, this was not important, and I could afford to follow my dream.

'Then within the space of about six weeks in September/ October 2020, the dream was taken from me. The way in which it was done made me feel rejected and left me bearing a strong resentment to the individuals who, as I felt, had sacrificed my job to help get themselves out of a financial calamity that was largely of their own making.'

Being receptive to wider opportunities is necessary when change is unwelcome and unexpected, as Peter discovered from first-hand experience:

'Whilst I was the curator at this air museum, I had dealings with two police officers who wanted to look into the possibility of setting up a small museum at the local police station. On hearing in early 2021 that I was now available, they invited me to become the curator of their new museum. This work is on a voluntary

unpaid basis as a police support volunteer and is now my principal occupation.

'I still maintain my own consulting business, though, and would use this as a vehicle for any future paid work if I could.

'I don't really consider myself as having properly retired, as I would go back to work if a suitable role came up. I would consider going back to another contract to work as curator at the museum I had invested so much time and passion in developing previously, but I would want to see major changes before I would even consider any offer. However, as this would take many years, returning to that role is unlikely to happen.'

The COVID-19 impact on the project was evident in the short and longer-term:

'In 2018, the aircraft museum secured significant National Lottery funding to go with about £1 million of its own match-funding (raised from grants and other sources) to finance the construction of a large, new aircraft hangar. Work began in late 2018 and continued until November 2019, after which came a period of intense activity during the museum's 2019/2020 winter closure period.

'This involved installing the new interpretation materials (display panels and showcases, to name a sample of what this entailed) as well as repositioning the entire aircraft collection.

'I had been heavily involved in designing all the new display materials and was also responsible for managing all the aircraft moves. The museum reopened on schedule in February 2020 but had to close due to the first COVID-19 Lockdown in March 2020, after just four weeks of opening.

'When the museum reopened after the first lockdown, visitor footfall was low, – as was the case for many venues. The reopening also coincided with final accounts demonstrating that

the potential risk to long-term opening was very apparent. In the necessary cost-cutting exercise that followed, my contract was terminated with a month's notice (in line with the terms of the contract). The events manager and learning officer were also both made redundant. We all left the museum's employment at the end of October 2020.'

Inspiration from another of 'Captain Tom's' generation, Peter recalls:

'It so happened that at this time, the museum's oldest volunteer steward was about to celebrate his one hundredth birthday in mid-November. At the museum AGM, he and his daughter announced to the meeting that he was launching a Facebook appeal to raise funds to enable the museum to keep the events manager and me in our jobs on a part-time basis for as long as possible. He was going to start this fund with a substantial personal donation.

'Over the next two months or so, the fund raised over £40,000 with donations coming from across the country: the BBC Local News team covered his birthday and the appeal, which led to substantial further donations.

'Not all monies were received via the Facebook appeal however, for example, the BBC could not identify the Facebook page explicitly and many donations were made via the Museum's website and ended up in the Museum's general fundraising account, although I continue to believe, especially given their timing, the intended destination of these donations was quite clear.

'The Museum Trustees however took a different view. Many other donors (including our one-hundred-year-old sponsor) had their donations returned. Attempts on our part to have the matter

investigated by the Fundraising Regulator and the Charities Commission came to nothing.

This incredible man (who is now one-hundred-and-one-years-old and still thankfully in good health) will have nothing further to do with the museum: both the events manager and learning officer left and found other jobs.'

'Being fifty-nine-years-old at the time all this happened, I decided that my 'least-worst' option was to activate my personal pension and live off that, either until another short-term job came along – or I gave up on the notion of working again.

'I decided that I would not attempt to find work for at least a year and spoke to some financial advisers, who calculated that I did not need to carry on working if I did not wish to. I had regarded the curator role as my 'dream job' and now that it had been taken from me, I had no motivation to go back to my earlier career path.'

When reflecting upon doubts or worries before or during making this leap, Peter recalls this as highly significant:

'Any other thoughts about my decision came more slowly. Retirement was not a path I chose, I lost my job and elected not to seek another one. I was ejected from a job that I wished to remain in for at least another three or four years and had no say in the matter.

'Initially, as realisation began to form, I felt angry and upset with the way in which I had been treated. I described the situation to fellow professionals, family, and friends in the same terms as I have used here, and all of them understood this view. It occupied most of my thoughts during waking hours and I did not sleep properly for several months.'

Positive experiences of this museum work, nevertheless, remain with Peter:

'Ever since I joined the museum as a volunteer in 2006, I have worked on the restoration of a 1950s aircraft of a type in which I have a particular interest, which has been a fascinating journey for me. I did very little work on the project when I was curator as I never had the time, but now I am starting to go back to the museum in my original role as a volunteer and am working on the project again.

'I am starting to regain my motivation for the work, and I also enjoy meeting the other volunteers again, where I feel that I am among friends.'

In considering obstacles and opportunities encountered, Peter reflects:

- *'I did not encounter any obstacles to the transition process itself.*
- *'Driven by the need to maintain an income stream with little chance of re-employment (this was in late 2020 when the museum / heritage industry was still in total lockdown and other avenues were not open to me), I started taking financial advice.*
- *'I met with two different advisers who looked at my circumstances and both advised that I had saved enough in my pension plan and other investments never to have to work again.*
- *'From then on it was a simple matter of picking the best financial plan and putting it into effect.*

'Whilst working at the museum, I had had dealings with two police officers of a local police station, who had conceived the idea of setting up a small exhibition in the foyer of the station, a building dating from the 1930s, which had strong links to the local aerospace industry. The primary audience for this small museum would be local school children.

'The police wanted to enlist my help and we had one or two meetings, including other stakeholders from the local university and the head teacher of a local school. Sadly, the COVID-19 lockdown prevented any progress on this scheme in 2020.

'Early in 2021, I sent an informal email to one officer, mainly to wish him a Happy New Year and enquire how his plans for the exhibition had progressed, if at all. He immediately responded with a request for an online meeting, in which he told me that he and another colleague had discovered the existence of four rooms in the building's basement which were currently used for storage, but which could be re-purposed to become a museum. It wouldn't be very big, but much larger than the original exhibition in the foyer.

'On learning that I was no longer at the Museum, I was invited to become a police support volunteer with the remit of setting up and curating this new museum. Very soon, we had developed outline plans for a museum that would enable the police to connect with primary school children and start to form relationships which would hopefully deter them from future criminal activities.'

'This idea of a 'museum with a message' fired my imagination and was instrumental in helping me to move on from the traumatic experience I had recently had with my previous employer.

'I can continue to use the heritage / curatorial skills that I had developed in three years of professional work at the other museum. As a chartered mechanical engineer, I also look forward to sharing my technical knowledge with school pupils for STEM (science, technology, engineering and mathematics) education projects.'

'During my time as a paid curator, I had started on a

professional qualification known as the Associateship of the Museums Association (AMA). This is a self-guided professional development programme run by the Association (the professional body for all UK museums and galleries) and is internationally recognised as a standard of excellence. At the point of leaving the aircraft museum, I had reached the final stage of the AMA programme, where I needed to undertake a project in collaboration with a museum.

'I am now documenting my work to establish the new museum as my museum curacy formal qualification project and am working with a mentor from another local museum to help me.'

Peter's lessons learned along the way which he feels would be helpful to share with others:

- *'Public sector employees can look forward to retiring at a known date with a known pension. Private sector employees cannot: in the private sector, you don't retire when you wish to stop working, you retire when your employer / client decides that he no longer has any use for your services. I have always known this would be the case, but it was still a shock when it happened as it did.*

- *'My own father worked for* forty *years for the same company and was 'offered early* retirement' against his will in the space of four weeks at the age of sixty-one when his company were closing the office where he worked and did not wish to take him to the new office. (They didn't tell him that that was the reason.) That was in 1988: I had no illusions about my 'dispensability' after that and had planned my finances accordingly. Over the next thirty-three years, always working in the private sector, I saw this sort of thing happen time and time again.

• 'For those of us not lucky enough to have a public-sector pension, the need to save for an independent pension is paramount, as private-sector occupational pensions are a thing of the past, and people these days can expect to change jobs many times in their careers.

• Hence, I would advise anyone starting out in their careers to get a personal pension sorted out as soon as possible, don't be tempted by employers' schemes and prioritise investment in their pensions over everything else in life wherever they can.

'I did all three of these throughout my career and as a result, I had a pension pot that could support me when the axe finally fell.'

Learning to fly again, Peter can share outcomes of his personal journey from which others can learn:

'Some things better, some things worse. Financially it's much the same – but with a slight gain as I am no longer paying personal pension contributions.

'I enjoy the freedom of not having to work, but that is balanced by an enduring sense of loss, having lost a job that didn't feel like work in the first place. I think that, overall, my sense of well-being has suffered.

'My curator job required contact with other people all day and every day, which I miss, as I live alone. Filling that void is sometimes difficult: I am not much of a 'joiner' and don't consider myself nearly old enough for the U3A (University of the Third Age) or Probus community yet!

'When the new museum gets properly established, this will be a great help.

'I am constrained by the amount of pension money I can draw down, at least in the first year or two, so money is slightly

tight unless I dip into my residual savings. It would be nice to be able to travel but I can't afford it. Current Covid restrictions make it impractical anyway, so I don't really have cause for complaint at present.

Looking to the future, Peter considers:

'I wouldn't say I am 'excited' for future opportunities, as I would much rather all this had never happened and that I was still in my pre-Covid employment.

'However, I'm very pleased that the new museum project offers me the chance to do something which will hopefully be meaningful and beneficial to the community. Without it, I think I would really struggle to make life meaningful and would probably end up doing a 'retired person's job', such as working in a shop or something. I don't quite view myself as 'retired', I see it more as having uncoupled my source of income from my source of work.

'What I can say is that I'm very pleased that I can combine my enthusiasm for engineering and my love of aviation history in this new venture. Communicating these two things to people (young and old) was one of the things I enjoyed most about my old job at the aviation museum, so I'm very glad that this is the part that I can most readily transfer to the new role.

'I may have lost the old job but perhaps I might have salvaged the best bit!'

Chapter 16

Family First: Shrey

Shrey is a dad to a son and a daughter and took the decision some years ago to step back from a career in computer programming, after successfully acquiring a master's degree. His priority since the age of thirty, when he made this defining decision, was to ensure he spent quality time with his beloved family beyond all other considerations. His overriding plan was to be available for his children in a way that would not have been possible in his last role.

Since then, having moved to a house chosen from plans opposite the site of the school he watched being built from the first piece of moved soil, he has been present for every step his children encountered, every milestone and celebration.

Whilst his wife is a long-term school governor, he has helped with hosting events at the school and within the community, photographing, not just the site development, but chronicling seasons and moments that marked the school for over sixteen years and counting! He unexpectedly fell seriously ill along the way, prior to the hindsight of COVID-19 owned by many of us in recent memory. This has given him cause to reflect on and review what constitutes success and routes to that aim not being linear nor uniform for all.

A quietly spoken gentleman with community and family as his champion causes, he has lived a life now long-term beyond lanyards as he retired at thirty from a formal working life as many might see that role. His legacy is the impact directly on his children and indirectly through their choices for a future awaiting them.

Shrey grew up in Kenya, moving to Britain in 1969 after his dad and sister passed away. He comments sagely about the expectations and ambitions of many families of Indian origin and how he combats that for his own children's work ethic by encouraging hard work, using their talents but also knowing that money alone is not a guaranteed road to fulfilment. Aspiration versus nepotism is something parents of many cultures, classes and races can create unrealistic expectations and division around, which Shrey's choices for his family have aimed to distinguish.

'I have a higher national diploma and a post graduate diploma in computer studies and a MSc in software engineering and I have worked as a computer programmer for all my working life. Since leaving work, I now mostly help family and friends with computer and software support in my own time. I am also a house husband with grown up children.

'Neither faith nor cultural influences really affected me at all. I'm not religious (even though I am a Jain), but I am more spiritual.

'What did motivate me was knowing that if I did not have a secure income from a place of work for when I have a family, then I needed to plan a way forward so that I would not be dependent on others.

'Hence investment for a longer-term future with choices within it was key: I wanted to have control of my future.

'I wanted to be a full-time parent and for us to be a full-time family. Whilst I love driving, especially when working in Windsor as the drive was an enjoyable part of my working experience, I hated the extended train commute into the centre of London daily.

'At times, there may have been fun aspects of my job but the

high risk of burn out is a known and very real possibility.

'Being fired from a high profile internationally reputed investment bank did me a favour; pushing me to leave being an employee behind and to start taking control of my own and our family's future.'

Shrey candidly reflects on the triggers personally or professionally, which made this plan a reality as being a combination of factors:

- *'Being 'passed over for promotion' even though I was the senior programmer.*

- *'New junior programmers were getting benefits like private health and more money than I was being offered at that time.*

- *'Having my position terminated despite doing my job well and with a higher understanding of specialist tasks such as 'commenting code' than peers, which they thought was time wasting. (I remember one day that the two other programmers were trying to figure out what a piece of code did. They spent the best part of the day each, so two working days between them, attempting to break that code. This could have been promptly sorted – if only whoever had written it had just spent five minutes putting comments in the code, to explain what was going on. However, they thought this approach was a waste of time and 'self-indulgent'). Technically, I was talking in code no one else understood, which was incredibly frustrating!*

- *'Lastly, when I was in a contracting capacity, my contract was renewed, but before starting the renewed contract, it was terminated for no reason. (The advantage of contracting work rather than permanent roles were just like a change of employer, but I could earn more money. Contractors got paid a lot more in those days and do so today. The nearest equivalent would be bank/agency staff in a care or health organisation or a supply teacher in schools).*

'I realised that control of my life and providing for my family was not in my hands. It was time to take control.

'This was long before the COVID-19 pandemic; it was in June 1999. One contract had finished. I had a week before I started the next contract at the same company, so we went on holiday and came back to my agent telling me that my contract had been cancelled. I already had everything in place to 'quit' working completely – so I did!'

When asked if Shrey had any doubts or worries before or during making this leap, he is clear that, because of the plans and investments and his wife's additional income and support, this was well thought through:

'None.

'The money I had earned was carefully invested and provided a good return. I had no mortgage nor any other debt, just the usual bills. My wife was working in the city for one of the top five professional accountancy services, which was, and remains, internationally acclaimed. After the birth of our first child in June 2001, she then returned three months after she took a year's maternity leave, having been an administrator there for a long time. By returning for three months and then leaving, she did not, therefore, need to pay back her maternity leave salary. Her income became additional collateral to go into our investments.'

As the plans fell into place:

- *'Initially I felt excited about my future!*
- *'As these plans were made because of my fellow professionals, I felt really happy that I would not have to see them again, to be honest.*
- *'In contrast, I was perfectly happy about telling my*

friends, although one asked, "What are you going to do? Won't you get bored?" Interestingly, I do not think this male friend would have asked a woman and mother the same thing, as gender role expectations were more stereotypical then, a time when the man in most homes was the so-called 'bread winner'. In many communities, that mindset is still very evident today. Ironically, however, when he later became a dad himself, he said to me one day, when explaining how much he was missing his own child growing up, "Now I get it."

• *'But I did feel nervous telling my mother. I think it was what would I do to keep me busy which was likely to be her concern, not if I had planned effectively through investments and preparation to provide for my family. However, she was diagnosed with cancer around July/August 1999, and she passed away in December 1999, so priorities were very different then. She so wanted to see the millennium, so we cremated her on the second of January, 2000.*

• *At a time of family bereavement and my leap to a new working role, it was a time of losses and new beginnings. I know she would have loved her grandchildren and spoilt them rotten. But to this day, my wife and I recall the winter months as a time we lost both our mothers and I became ill: it simply reaffirms the importance of family bonds and the reason for my decision to do what I did.*

• *'Perhaps, also, I am influenced by many of my wider family being long termly financially affluent when living in Kenya, but I saw more than once that money doesn't go with you when you die, and I believe family values are more important.*

• *'Most people were very supportive. No one had any advice, as no one had done anything like this before. Some friends did say I should do this or that, but as they did not have*

160

any experience in what I was doing, it was not very helpful.

'I wanted to enjoy a life with balance: whilst my predecessors made their fortune in Kenya, I warned my son to assume that double the amount of money will be required for any new resource and for both of my children to do something they love in the workplace.

'Our family ethics and moral code has strengthened in my own journey.

'They might as well do something they love as work and already my eldest is encouraged to plan for when is it enough and how will life be sustainable when working full time is not a necessity. That choice is more important, if carefully planned, than huge amounts in the bank you never get time off to enjoy!'

In considering if there were any organisations, resources or training which proved useful in supporting your change of work life, Shrey recalls:

'No. Nobody, that I was aware of had actually done what I did when I retired at thirty.

'I became really good at using Photo and image related applications. All was learnt with books and magazines. This was all before YouTube and fast internet, which we take for granted today!

'If I was to do this journey starting today, the internet is full of advice, which could be a positive tool, but there is also much which is conflicting and without real people's advice from experience. Hence my willingness to support this document alongside others who have chosen a different path to their initial plan or destiny. Technology opens many windows for information, but too much of something is not a good thing.'

'I had no pension, believing I was way too young for that! I

did, however, have income from investments. I know a really good financial advisor who has always done the best for me. I already knew I could survive and have a good life with the income.'

In terms of any obstacles encountered, Shrey considers:

'My wife and I just did things as they needed to be done, addressed any unexpected hiccoughs as they arose. There was no real routine, to begin with. We shared what we had to do and continue to do that even now. We take up each other's slack. We both share chores. Whoever gets to the hoover first! Most importantly, we both continue to support each other.

'A few years before my wife's mum passed away, she was diagnosed with a mental illness. This required my wife to support her mum at home, then in hospital and lastly in her care home, where she passed away. I got on with everything else. The kids and their Kumon tutorials, dinner and other after-school events. This replicated the way my wife took over when I was recovering. It was just done. We were a team then and now, picking up the slack when needed without being asked.'

Life sends us curve balls and Shrey recalls his:

'On 6th or 7th October, 2016, I woke up with excruciating pain in my right foot near the arch. I could not put any pressure at all on that foot. I managed to get an appointment with my GP and he prescribed me a strong anti-inflammatory and said I had gout. We celebrated my wife's fiftieth birthday on 8th October and all was well. A few weeks went by and the gout had returned, meaning I was back to GP and received another prescription. By the end of October, I was starting to feel very flu-like: hot, cold, tired and achy. Looking back at photos of that time, I now recognise I did not look well.

'I was taking cold and flu medication which didn't really work. Then, at one in the morning, I got myself up and collapsed on the sofa, but could not get a GP to come out, so after a day or so, I had enough strength to make it to the GP where the usual checks were carried out and I was referred for a blood test. Sometime around then, I collapsed in the bathroom, my wife remembers me having a seizure as she and my son looked on. The GP called following the blood test results and told me to come in immediately. They knew something was wrong.: on the twenty-fourth November, I was admitted to the acute cardiac unit.

'After a lot of tests and prodding and probing, they concluded I had bacterial growth on my mitral valve, causing my flu and gout-like symptoms. The condition was called endocarditis.

'I had two options, but rather than managing through medication and deferring an operation, due to the extensive damage, it was recommended that I was young enough to recover fully from a valve replacement.

'First at our local hospital for two weeks, before being transferred to The Royal Brompton Hospital, where the surgery was performed, for two weeks and then back at our local hospital for a final two weeks. I returned home with a six-week course of antibiotics on a drip to clear any remnants of the infection.

I was back home and in a lot of pain. That went mostly after two months. I still get the odd pain here and there. It was then that it hit me I had survived open heart surgery! In hospital, I was just going through the motions. Doctors explaining what they were going to do, sign here, facing the reality was a shock '...

'It was while recovering at The Royal Brompton Hospital that I came to the realisation that life is too short. Just get on with whatever you want to do even if it just sitting around doing nothing. Get rid of the people who take you down, the negativity of those people.

'My phone book has gotten a lot smaller.

'Having said that, we have some amazing friends. They dropped everything when both our mums died, they looked after our children and bought food. One friend sat with my wife at The Brompton for over five hours while I was being taken apart and put back together. That still gets to me, even after all this time.

'In hindsight, my philosophical perspective on life deepened as a result of this illness and the guidance and support I give my children has a more holistic approach than it did before. As much as the drugs and medical expertise, I also owe my recovery, and increased reflective approach, to an inspirational fellow patient in the next bed. He was someone I would never have met if it wasn't for this experience and he enabled me to reflect now on this time of pain and high risk, as one where laughter was shared and an inspirational Irish Guard, with a loud voice and direct approach, made the time not just bearable but enriched. Having recently heard he has since passed away this is a fitting tribute to the man who was larger than life and made the hell of that time bearable at The Brompton.

'Before becoming ill, I made a document called 'Read Me First', listing just a few passwords and stuff that my wife and kids may need to know. I got the idea from a friend whose father had passed away recently but had completed his paperwork so nothing would be left to do when he went unexpectedly.'

What would Shrey like others to remember?
- 'Now what is my advice? Live life to the full. Don't leave it until tomorrow.
- Being an example that my children can follow, not just talk about it: it is my focus. To teach and encourage them as I go. Help them follow their dreams.'

Shrey enjoys utilising so many skills from his previous working role. In fact, he believes all of them have relevance and usefulness today:

'I still enjoy 'tinkering' with computers and technology. I like being efficient. Doing repetitive things only once. I will spend the time to do it better, requiring more effort in the short term, but less effort long term.'

He loves keeping up with the latest technology. Improving his photography skills and post-processing skills (now with help from his son who utilises photography in a professional capacity). He still does a bit of consultancy work in helping friends with their IT issues which again supports those transitional skills beyond the formal working environment.

Further lessons learned along the way Shrey feels would be helpful to share with others include the following:

- *'Figure out what you want to achieve and focus on it every day.*
- *'The universe will provide the means for you to achieve what you want even though it may not look like it.*
- *'Recognise that everything happens for a reason – good or bad – and make it work for you i.e. 'own it.'*

Life changed for Shrey for the better overall as he explains:

'Yes, most definitely yes! I am happy. I am where I want to be. I might sometimes miss some of the social aspects of working, but not enough to replace them.

'I am able to spend all my time with my family and friends. As a family, we can go on longer holidays, not just the two weeks. And just do nothing if I feel like it. Daily there is less stress, such as going shopping during the daytime and not at the weekends when it's less busy!

Shrey celebrates a richness in shared family experiences with life-long memories forged. Board games and movies on a trip to Lancashire simply as a change of scene, modelling healthy balance for his son with an intense commitment to work projects recently. He advocates a need for balance.

'We love Orlando and Disney. We've been going every two years since 2004 when we bought into the Disney Vacation Club. In 2019, we went to Singapore and Phuket, Thailand. We want to do that again. Singapore and somewhere else in the far east, such as Bali and other parts of Thailand and Malaysia. Can't wait to get back to that!'

On reflection, Shrey considers what he knows now, that he wishes that he knew when he first made this change to working life.

- *'Make goals and stick to them.*
- *'Talk to people who are where you want to be in life. Find out how they got there and follow their advice.*
- *'Be aware of other opportunities as well. One thing could lead to other possibilities that you had never thought of.*

'After all, you would not take driving lessons from someone who could not drive?'

Final advice for those embarking on a career change or working regime?

- *'Just go for it. Something good will come out of it, even if you thought you had made a mistake. Have faith and think positively.*
- *'I found that a university education is not essential to become a success. Even though I have a few qualifications, the most useless one was the MSc. A lot of wasted time and money and held back my career instead of propelling it further. Every employer had said to me, 'So, you haven't been working for the last year?' And I'm saying, 'But I have a MSc in software engineering.'*

• Prime example: my son. Only studied up to A'level. He decided not to pursue university applications as he was immediately working doing what he loves. He has taken advice from me and his bosses, both of which are self-made and very successful. How many twenty-year-olds do you know have bought their first car brand new? In his case, he will be buying a Porsche Caymen by the end of this year or early next year. He set a goal about two years ago that he would have this car by the end of this year. He is debt free and had no student loans, unlike all of his friends who are at university.'

Shrey remains very clear that university has its place, but it is not for everyone. He cites many examples internationally known, including Steve Jobs who never finished university, whilst Bill Gates dropped out of Harvard. Meanwhile, Ray Krock made McDonald's a household name and what it is today when he was in his fifties. And there are many others.

He is clear that everything happens for a reason, – good or bad. We just don't necessarily know why at the time. Take it on faith. He advocates, you always get what you need and not what you want. If you are fortunate, what you want is also what you need.

Here is someone happy with his decisions and proud of his family unit. He celebrates opportunities for lots of travelling (when we can, before and post COVID-19) and learning about other cultures.

Chapter 17

'Tell Me It's Not True…' From Stage to Staffroom: Cate

On first meeting this lady on day one of an extended piece of training led by the Royal Opera House, her energy crackled and her passion for the arts was a catalyst for those around her. Cate's down-to-earth approach then truly undersold what a plethora of skills she had and oh, what a journey of self-discovery she has undertaken! This has fully utilised her varied performance skills, to enhance her professional and indeed personal achievements.

A scholarship girl, who went to a school and fell in love with choral singing in a cathedral, she also sang at bus stops in her early teens with the expectation of one day being discovered and propelled to a career where her talents would be applauded. Cate's love of music and performance radiates from her.

Of course, she was 'discovered' and was able to fulfil her dream to perform professionally but what she does now is enable discovery of the arts in secondary education, where it can otherwise be marginalised and underfunded.

Currently, a teacher with much responsibility for the arts – including teaching A' Level Art which she will admit had never previously been part of her expected skillset – I later learned of Cate's commitment to Stagecoach (workshops for young people in singing, drama and dance) over her weekends. Later still, her involvement in her church youth work provision has been driven by her creativity and faith to support an ever-wider reach through her provision. She combines a passion for creativity with an altruistic commitment beyond her working role, to support her community whenever the opportunity arises.

Cate runs at one hundred miles an hour juggling a career, family and supporting young people through her faith and passion for performing and creative enterprise as an outlet for expression. She also has a business for home spa experiences, which was a treat to explore during COVID-19 Lockdown as we all discovered Zoom becoming the new way to meet up and enjoy new experiences. Her interpersonal skills make all this work, but our friendship forged as a longer-term commitment over more than one lunch or cocktail shared, and a shared love of *Blood Brothers. I have seen this favourite gritty musical set in Liverpool at least nine times: Cate was in the cast ... a fact which still leaves me in awe!*

What is clear is that Cate juggling family and career has meant, more than once, stopping to change path and taking that leap into the unknown for a number of reasons. Her very realistic reflections on that journey are grounded in a clear message showing that such a leap is not always easy in the short term and is certainly not glamorised as a 'road to Damascus' moment where everything is right with her choice and outcome. However, a life well lived, whilst sometimes messy or muddled at times, also offers opportunities if we have the courage to take that leap.

This lady has that courage.

'I was an actor/ musician initially. I completed my training at Mount View and struggled a bit to get paid work, to begin with. (To this day, this organisation promotes a promise for successful

entrants to be 'a performance and creative learning centre of excellence and opportunity for all' with a reputation for extended training for careers in theatre as a 'world-leading drama school.)'

'I had an agent and was auditioning for roles with several 'call backs' but whilst success was tangible, it remained elusive at that time. I went to some pretty disheartening open auditions as well, where I vividly remember, on one occasion, being rejected in the queue without even performing!

'When I finally got a tour, it was so exciting! We were taking Brecht's Happy End to Clwyd Theatr Cymru and touring around Wales. It was everything I had trained for.

'That was then: now I am now a music teacher and middle leader in a secondary school.'

Whilst initially fulfilling her long-term dream, Cate began to realise not all was as she had imagined it to be – and choices needed to be made.

'A variety of triggers influenced my leaving the acting profession. The main one was that I met my now husband when I was at drama school. We moved in together just before I went on tour. But after several months of just seeing each other at weekends, he said this wasn't really what he wanted: I had a difficult decision to make.

'However, what I had also realised was that actually, the touring life was not something I really enjoyed. The rehearsal process was great – and probably the first couple of weeks of the show were exciting, but thereafter it was the same night after night.

'Staying in digs with the cast members created a camaraderie, but it was a lot of drama off stage too! Working life *was a bit back to front starting at five p.m. and finishing at eleven o'clock in the evening, meaning I'd still be up at a reasonable hour with not a lot to do. It's also quite an expensive lifestyle as well, as, despite public perception at times, wages weren't great and you're paying quite a lot for meals out and other additional expenses, as you don't have the equipment to cook for yourself.*

'So, when presented with an ultimatum, it wasn't really a difficult decision.

'My journey into teaching was quite a roundabout journey. I already taught singing at a Saturday theatre school since leaving drama school and continued this commitment right up until the present day as I really enjoyed this. I also taught piano and clarinet. I had a variety of temporary jobs whilst auditioning, which led me to St Ann's Hospital in Tottenham.

'After finishing my theatre tour, I took in a permanent role there as mental health act coordinator. This work was really interesting, and I particularly enjoyed the training element which involved running courses on the Mental Health Act for hospital staff social services. I then moved into working as an office manager for a charity that offered psychotherapy for young people.

'Meanwhile, I continued instrumental teaching after work.

'After the birth of my second child, I reassessed my life and priorities:

- *'We had moved house and the commute into London was no longer feasible.*

- *'Childcare was too expensive for two children under three for my husband and me to be paying for that amount of commuting travel.*

- *'The year my son turned three, I trained as a teacher. Maybe it seems mad to attempt that when my children were both under five, – but one way or another, we managed.*

'My parents had always said since I was young that I would be a great teacher, but I wanted to be a star! Isn't it funny how things turn around? I'm glad I have that theatre experience and the roles I undertook before retraining to become a teacher. I am equally glad that, as well as doing all this, I then chose a different life. In fact, I think that life experience within the arts has helped me as a teacher and certainly means I am informed about the industry many of my students wish to embark on.

'I try not to think about my parents being right, however!'

Whilst COVID-19 didn't instigate this leap to a new career, it has influenced Cate's perception of her current role and other aspects of her life:

'Covid did not impact this decision but has seen me thrive and then struggle with this career choice. Also, it did provide me with an opportunity to think about teaching as a vocation and adapt to provide online teaching resources and lessons, with often challenges of engaging the most vulnerable children. Those who needed self-expression through the arts most, often felt adrift from access to the bedrock of this support: school. Setting the year eleven students off into the world with so much left undone was really tough for them and for me.

'I also used this time to develop my spa and well-being business in the evenings, not just to raise some additional revenue but as a social outlet and to connect those at home not able to socially meet and enjoy a treat.'

When reflecting on any doubts or worries before or during making this leap, Cate recalls this happened a lot:

'All the time!

'Even now I wonder if I'd like to 'tread the boards' again – but I love my job. Teaching often feels like a battle I cannot win and it can be soul-destroying on a bad day as it takes and takes and takes: sometimes it feels that it doesn't give back.

'Nevertheless, when I doubt myself, I think I've already had three careers, I don't know what else I can do... or even if I can bear to go through the whole process again.'

Feelings when undergoing the change from one career to the next were strong:

'Making the decision to leave acting was so hard as it was my dream.

'I wasn't sure, by any means, and I was certainly angry at being forced to make the choice between my husband and acting. I sought support from the cast at the time, helping me talk through options and plans. This was easier than if I had been an employee of a corporate company as I was ultimately self-employed, this meant it was not an issue announcing my decision to fellow professionals.

'My friends and family were fully supportive of the decision to leave acting and were very pleased when I decided to train as a teacher.

'On reflection from within my place of work and my social and family network, I had plenty of different people providing a sounding board or listening ear, often with different perspectives on the issues this raised, which was helpful, especially as I didn't have access to organisations, resources or training which proved useful in supporting my change of work-life.'

The pros and cons of the retraining experience were as follows:

'Financially, it was a struggle to retrain at that point, especially with two very young children. We managed – but it was

173

tough. I took a route into teaching which, due to my prior qualifications was paid, but not lucratively so. The wage from my graduate teacher programme just about covered our childcare. But as others will say, I am sure, you just always somehow manage to get by.

'Moreover, because of my experience, I was very quickly promoted to the head of department position. Therefore, that initial short-term pain soon reaped rewards financially.'

New skills and how were these acquired:

'I had to train as a teacher and that's a whole new skill set as you are never done with learning. There really is no other profession that beats itself with a stick forever asking, how can I do better?

'But there's something exciting about us learning.

'I did this as part of the GTP scheme through Bedfordshire's SCITT, a kind of apprenticeship model into teaching.'

When considering which skills were transferrable from theatre to classroom arenas, Cate is very clear:

- *'All of them!*
- *'Understanding the performing arts industry helps with my delivery of content-and also in career guidance.*
- *'Working with mental health previously, this is now a huge influence on my current role.*
- *'It also supports me to support my students not only holistically but is a great help now (due to staffing shortages) that I have to teach health and social care.*
- *'My experience of writing fundraising applications and successful lottery bids has helped me with finding additional funding for poorly financed departments, providing an improved experience for the students.'*

Life has changed for Cate and her family in obvious and subtler ways:

'Well, I have a rewarding career that is both exhilarating and frustrating in equal measure. No two days are the same and I love that.

'Financially, – well, in theory I'm better off – but hey, you always live up to your means, don't you?

'It has enabled me to spend time with my children during the school holidays and I now support my brother with looking after my nieces too.

'But I miss performing. I got my kicks out of teaching at the drama school for years, but I have given this up in favour of having my weekends back very recently. I do think that I might do little amateur dramatics in the future though.'

As her teaching career progresses, she realises that teaching has its challenges and that more of the aspects of the role are ever prevalent, but the balance works:

'Ha - marking! Teaching is bloody hard, and it doesn't get any easier.

'It has been a crazy time in all schools and my experience is typical of many as we leave the pandemic behind in the wider society.

'Preparation for Ofsted means both the work and pressure are full-on and COVID-19 related absences mean all of the cover for classes needs to be constantly juggled.

'So please don't choose a career in teaching if you are expecting an easier time than in your current role: but the pluses are significant.

'Seriously though, spending time with my family is something I would not have had if I had continued in theatre.'

Advice for those embarking on a career change or working regime is clear from Cate:

- *'If you aren't happy, 'get your brave on' – and make the change.*
- *'Say yes to opportunities and yes to help when it is offered.'*

PART 3:

'Hello from the Other Side'. Experiences, Pitfalls, Transferrable Skills from Case Studies.

Pearls of wisdom from those who have taken the leap – and learned to fly.

Chapter 18

Working and Thinking Differently. Transferrable Skills and Their Application, from Those Who Have Taken 'That Leap'

Sometimes, it isn't just about skills and competencies, *but also about marketing those attributes, so that they are transparently transferrable to new roles and responsibilities, beyond our initial professional occupation.*

The acronyms and hidden, as well as obvious norms of any professional role, can blur understanding and set expectations off at a tangent to what reality is.

An example might be:

'I fancy retraining to be a teacher! After all, I supported my child through her home learning during the COVID-19 Pandemic and to start at nine a.m. and end just after three p.m. with long holidays... how difficult could it be?'

The case studies including Cate and Florence would have something to say about that, as would Sharon and Sara, an array of talented individuals who either left teaching and class-based careers, or in fact chose to join later in their professional journey!

Sometimes we can undersell what we already do which is relevant, transferrable and, indeed, *innovative in a new environment.*

The organisational skills from PW, Alan or Peter, were common-place expectations in the Navy, engineering or the corporate world. Also, in banking roles at a senior level, it is only when you enter a place of work where they are not embedded, that the value of such skills are evidently clearer. Likewise, from the corporate or public sector, the armed forces to our wonderful NHS, taking the leap to self-employed status, means there isn't that 'safety net' of infrastructure to support you as previously often taken for granted. Hence assurances and due diligence are necessary to protect yourself and ensure consultancy is well matched with clear expectations of those trading a service – *and those paying for expertise!*

I certainly fell foul of initially thinking *if I was not representing my previous organisation, then I could not possibly charge similar hourly or daily rates for consultancy.* I quickly learned that is not the case and listened to others who suggested a sliding scale of charges from one off pieces of work, a selection of tasks over an agreed period of time and an incentive-led extended contractual rate, for commitment over ten days. This may also, in the early days, have a buffer for friends or start-up opportunities, but as PW demonstrated, such rates can be reviewed and renegotiated. *Remember to consider your own USPs (unique selling points) and confidently stand by those.*

Misused skills and capabilities around shared language, and what key terms mean, can result in communication issues becoming a barrier, not an enabler.

One example of this is when I was working as a county adviser for personal, social and health education and later, as a head teacher following the tragic death of Victoria Climbie. This serious case review resulted in a nationwide shared response of multi-professional training entitled 'Every Child Matters.' Working within mixed professional teams was crucial, as the inquiry pulled no punches in publicising that the number of agencies working with this family and who were assumedly responsible for keeping this little girl safe, failed her. This was ultimately due to a reprehensible lack of joined-up thinking and sharing of information in a way that could keep this child safe. During such training, I realised something as simple as the word 'register' had significantly different connotations across professional fields that were all supporting the same children and their safeguarding needs. For example:

- For a teacher, a register marked attendance or lack of it, the absence patterns and frequency often became a red flag for early concerns.

- For the social worker, this word is linked to a child protection register, meaning there is a history of significant harm in the family or specifically in a child's history.

- For a nurse, it may mean links to specific clinician input which could throw up all sorts of issues to do with that child's needs now and prior to that discussion taking place.

Thinking of the tragic outcome for many children who sadly are lost even today, despite being known to multiple organisations due to safeguarding concerns and how messages were missed then, and continue to be, reaffirms to me how essential it is for everyone to have a clear and shared language.

Proven transferrable skills listed in a checklist:
Using the information already shared by me and our twelve case studies, it is hoped there might be 'nuggets' of information which may determine possible new ventures where your transferrable skills are best matched. *These are not from*

celebrities, but ordinary people, demonstrating extraordinary capacity for navigating change management. All of these have been generous in sharing their stories of inspiring lives beyond lanyards, that ensured success and fulfilment followed.

Likewise, gaps in our skillsets may not necessarily be areas of weakness but may encourage a systematic approach to additional training or buying in expertise, such as bookkeeping or legal advice.

Questions arising during that leap to life beyond lanyards may therefore include:

- What do you have in your 'professional portfolio'?
- What is embedded and what needs sharpening up?
- What are the gaps – and will these matter in your chosen next step?

Here is a self-assessment tool, using the expertise of our case studies and a few additional options from me for good measure, which aims to support the planning around viable next steps. After all, prior knowledge is always a bonus, just as the early explorers who sailed to the edge of the map of the 'Known World' back in history said, *'Beware, there be dragons ahead!'*

Remember, if you are looking to provide pastoral service training through a local authority, you may not need accounting skills or be able to sing, act or play multiple instruments like Cate. However, as Sara and Tom found, creative expertise was valued in their new roles, alongside organisational expertise and communication aptitude above all else. *In contrast, to be an astronaut the role won't require you to create musical scores, but an aptitude for mathematics and science need to be clearly show cased, as might Darren's off-the-scale IQ!*

First thoughts which come to mind are:

- To set up your own business, don't simply offer every aspect of your previous career, *as you will spend too much time doing the things you wanted to leave behind.*
- Instead, focus on the parts of the job you loved to provide a service which is of interest to you as much as it is of value to someone else.

As a result, on a personal level, I have determined, I don't want to yet again step into a school with a gap in current headship, nor do I want to commit to Mondays and Fridays as a regular expectation. *I certainly feel thirteen Ofsted inspections are enough for anyone and whilst all successful – and great as a 'lose weight quick' solution in my case – I really don't want that stress any more!*

What I enjoyed most was building teams, executive coaching, training and enrichment projects, hence I have become braver at saying no thank you to projects not with this focus – and found that alone rather empowering!

Actually, I am beginning to like term time breaks away, so contracts without the flexibility of when I work and how (including remote access balanced with on-site commitments are also not reaffirming my life-work balance in this new chapter. Perhaps what has surprised me most is that interested parties are happy to accept all of those terms, if the partnership is well matched.

It is also useful to talk to those who knew you professionally, within your team and from a more strategic perspective: their answers may surprise you. You could ask them:

- What did you consider to be my greatest strengths?
- What seemed to motivate me, or make me the happiest?
- What areas do you think I should avoid as others have since shown better ways of fulfilling this part of the role?

- What part of my professional role would you pay for a fellow professional?
- What did I do that caused unnecessary work or stress to others? *A brave question but with distance to alleviate pride and ego, a useful piece of feedback to continue to grow your own knowledge of self!*

One option is to give, before you take the leap, a three-hundred-and-sixty-degree survey to a number of professional partners. There are plenty on the internet, free and at a cost, but it may be useful to employ a middle person such as a coach to work through the outcomes as it can be whether positive or negative feedback, an emotive but powerful piece of work.

Another consideration is such reviews give reflection time for the person responding and distance from you, so that feedback might be more honest and less softened as might be the case in a direct conversation with some involved in this process? No doubt the truth is, just as the case studies shared within these pages began with a questionnaire, these were developed using further email and face to face or telephone conversations. *Hence the best option is probably a mix of both strategies.*

I have completed, for Master's Post Graduate level of further study, a number of three hundred and sixty degree surveys for others - and gone through them myself, always finding them useful. Likewise, a series of open questions as received with responses from Royal Opera House Leaders for Impact, showed me that the contributors recognised me as a person as well as a professional: but accepted at some point, I would move on. This empowered much of my succession planning and exit strategy.

So, what can you bring to the table?

What now follows is a list of what have been recognised as

transferrable skills mentioned to date from my journey and that of our case studies, for you to consider:

- What you have.
- What needs developing against your researched next steps and advertised person specifications?
- And what is irrelevant at this time.

This way, next steps may include further training either brokered through a reputable provider or indeed, via the 'University of World Wide Web Search' for additional advice, training and tutorials. Attainable next steps then become more focussed and avoid anyone becoming overwhelmed. and side-tracked into training and expense which is unnecessary.

Likewise, let's learn from Darren in his journey from a plumber to a priest or Tom, from West End musical director to a more local and community-based role, to, most importantly to follow a faith-led vocation or to enrich family life, respectively. Many people, through the COVID-19 pandemic, have extended expertise in a long-held hobby or taken up a new skill or interest. Thinking back to Shrey's philosophy which has encouraged his own children to not just think of school followed by university as an only route to success and happiness. Indeed, in the months writing and researching this book, not only has his son bought the car of his dreams aged twenty-one and launched some incredible photographs for an internationally acclaimed sports car brand, his youngest child has achieved some of the best A' Level results for her school but to date, continues to develop her Etsy based jewellery design interest. *One size most certainly does not fit all.*

Let's, therefore, encourage ourselves to keep an open mind set and to review our competencies and skills within, but also beyond, the previous workplace, enabling people to begin a new business in garden therapy, jewellery design and renting out wedding accessories, to name just a few brave new leaps into new ventures, all harnessing aptitude, and skills completely different from our previous lives.

The most poignant example I know of this is my own dad: previously in a very senior role which at times combined high level pressure and responsibility through his hugely successful career. Now, over eighty he has discovered a love of carving wood, creating items to fundraise for charities and a local museum. However, this outlet also enables him to meet other men of a similar age, to focus on a task whilst enjoying much-valued companionship and peer-to-peer learning... *As Tom and Darren explained, monetary rewards may be necessary to some extent, but need not be the main drivers for some people.*

What follows doesn't intend to be an exhaustive list, but a summary common to myself and/ or most case studies shared – or specific to a particular person included within these pages.

Transferrable skills: relevant to my chosen next career flight.

Skill	A strength	Some experience of	A training need	Not relevant
People skills: *ease when talking to lords, ladies, children to elderly and everyone in between.*				
Resilience				
Determination to overcome obstacles.				
Strong work ethic				
Application of new technology				
Knowledge of managing HR issues				
Policy development				
Knowledge of legal parameters				
Public relations on a national and potentially international scale				
Ability to delegate				
Working with mental health previously				
Mental health expertise				
Writing fundraising applications and successful lottery bids				

Understanding the performing arts and industry.				
Delivery of content in a motivational/marketable way				
Experience managing conflict				
Solution-based thinking				
Ability to prioritise				
Effective time management				
Interpersonal skills				
Experienced communicator				
Experience leading appraisals				
Career guidance for others.				

Evidence of successful Teamwork: **quality of work you produce together: examples.**

Skill	A strength	Some experience of	A training need	Not relevant
An open mind and a positive attitude				
Professionally manage difficult and challenging behaviours				
Excellent listening skills				
Giving regard to issues of confidentiality				
Able to work co-operatively and collaboratively with other disciplines				
Organisational skills				
Public speaking confidence				
Negotiating skills *and diplomacy!*				
Writing reports.				
Goal focussed				
Ambitious. *Wanting to be the best at what you do*				

Accurate record keeping				
Professionalism: examples				
Training and development evidenced				
Generic Management skills				
Academic rigour				
Broad interests beyond the workplace				
Sense of fun				
Lots of good ideas				
Desire to constantly improve				
Positive mental attitude				
Flexibility				
Playing a musical instrument				
Good general knowledge				
Being a good role model				
Financial expertise				
Experience of managing press				
Confident use of social media				

Marketing experience				
Creativity: *ability to think outside the box!*				
Patience: did this come up in your three sixty reviews or references?				
Excellent memory				

What I soon realised is for anyone embarking on a change of career, planned or otherwise, you will probably have many more transferrable skills and expertise than you imagine. It is also notable that as well as transferrable skills, capacities and capabilities are also intertwined. Different perspectives within this list are partly personality based but also driven by the strategic planners versus the more creative individuals drawn upon in our sample of successful professionals.

Indeed what also becomes apparent from completing this checklist, sometimes, the new learning arising from gaps in your professional portfolio, can, in fact, be part of the greatest and most rewarding aspects of taking that leap. Who can forget Darren's journey from plumber to priest? With no university education and a dyslexia diagnosis during this remarkable transition, it was only through the additional assessments that he discovered he had an exceptionally high IQ.

The workplace is changing dramatically, and our skills and personal attributes will enrich current and future opportunities to work, learn and enrich our lives from a broader and more interesting baseline than simply those with aptitude to complete certain exams at the age of sixteen, eighteen *or indeed other any age!*

Chapter 19

A Route Map from Fellow Travellers: Trip Adviser for Those Planning to Fly

Ego States are consistent patterns of feeling, thinking and behaviour that we all possess. These are significant, I believe, in 'life beyond lanyards' and, at times, we can all find ourselves susceptible to all possibilities. Transactional Analysis identifies these three Ego States as Parent, Adult, and Child.

In the 1950s, Eric Berne developed the idea that people can switch between different states of mind. Sometimes this can be in the same conversation and in different parts of their lives, including at work as well as at home. His suggestions emerged from his observations of people in his own clinical practice:

- The Child State consists of parts of ourselves which have resonance with our childhood. *It is childlike but not childish* with evidence of intuition, creative and spontaneous drive and enjoyment.

- The Parent state demonstrates that, over years, we absorb influences from our actual parents and also from authority figures such as teachers, bosses and role models. It has two functions:

- To enable people to be better actual parents of their own children.

- To enable many responses to life to be made automatically: 'that's the way it's done'.

• As a result, the Adult is freed from making decisions which, on a scale of importance, are low.

• The Adult state is where we aspire to act when fully mature, demonstrated in the effective navigation of challenges in modern life. It can also regulate the activities of the Parent and Child at times, using mediation.

When we are young, we look up to our elders, those with responsibility and we don't doubt that they have all the answers and know how to do the right thing. That is typical of any parent-to-child relationship and often the case for child-to-adult.

According to my dad, for me, it was after the age of about six, when he was disappointed to notice that I had stopped saying 'Yes, Daddy.' Prior to this milestone, believing my Dad who was my role model knew everything and was always right, questions and challenges, alongside doubt and uncertainty had not been part of my expectation. A perfect parent/ child relationship at that time perhaps, as no doubt reflected in holiday photos, videos and, dare I say, ciné films of smiling birthdays and Christmases over that time? I am sure I am not alone in this idyllic catalogue being often faded or out-of-focus imagery of that era! I accept I was lucky to have this experience as many don't, but when the ego states change, it is not without casualties.

I was clearly precocious beyond my years when, aged seven, the phrase, 'Yes, Daddy,' was allegedly replaced by a bold, singular word, 'Why?' Shortly after this transitional stage, I apparently learned to roll my eyes and perfected a look of utter disdain to anyone who thought differently to me or told me they knew best. I remember refusing a lift from school as my mother had chosen a radically short haircut, *but looking back at 1970s fashion, never once did I consider that, seeing some of my outfits, she may have, in fact, been rather uncomfortable with being seen with me!* Moreover, looking now at photos of my Mum at that time, she owned a confidence and 'sassiness' that was impressive, but teenage angst meant I didn't want any of my family to stand out too much! *Isn't hindsight a wonderful thing?*

During our adolescence, we pivot from assertive confidence to huge introspection and self-doubt. That joyous unchallenged belief that all would be well – whatever decision we made, *so long as the choices we made came from a good place* – gets whisked into a hormonal and emotional maelstrom, forging much of our teenage experience. At that point, the last thing we often deliberately choose to do is listen and act always on the sound advice of others; especially if they have an adult-to-child relationship with us.

This falls back neatly, I believe, to having relevance when we leave a career by choice – or also as Peter explained, beyond our decision. Child, adult, and parent ego states can be at play in our responses within the same day, depending on our level of confidence in a new situation, compared to the terror of the unknown and often unclear future.

I heard many times how my father left the Merchant Navy, joined the police and secured a varied and successful career. However, I can honestly say that whilst I heard the ending of that chapter for him*, I question now whether I really listened to the vastness of that future without uniform, public standing, rank and routine.* In fact, perhaps it is more that whilst I *did listen*, maybe I didn't absorb this with empathy of having 'walked that walk.'

Now I understand.

I remember him saying when he first walked into a small cottage on the south coast, no longer married, children grown up and retired from a life of excitement, challenge and dramatic opportunities, he opened the door with keys fresh from the estate agent and listened… to the silence. In that soundless void, at that moment came a loud crash of reality, as the question he had avoided until that moment, albeit unconsciously, was 'Who am I?' By that, he didn't mean his name or whether he still looked like his passport photograph - or had changed his biometric or physical identity, but perhaps more profoundly it meant, 'Who am I *now, not just today, but tomorrow and going forward?* He recognised, 'I have been a husband, son, sibling, father, boss, ambassador… *but what constitutes the essence of me now,* when all those roles are, in fact, obsolete at worst, or, at least, minimal, as life has moved on?'

What was he left to be at that point when the professional and personal roles and responsibilities were stripped bare – and what has changed now? Well, he retired and remarried and lived happily and quietly, with a beautiful sea view. However, a life beyond lanyards, as Peter, Sara and other case studies have explained, is not always linear. To get to that point where his identity was regrown and completed beyond retirement, my Dad:

- Initially delivered Meals on Wheels and joined the local town council. *Never underestimate the value of voluntary roles to come down from the full time busy working diary, but to fuel your self-worth and forge new relationships.*

- He became a game keeper for a while, as it came with accommodation and reaffirmed a love of country living.

- He renovated a building he bought as a shell and made it into a welcoming home.

- He paid a plasterer by the hour to teach him that skill, so that he could complete the task himself from then on.

- He set up an owners' club for a favourite type of car to meet people with a shared love of motoring.

- He met with 'Old Men at the Harbour' to 'tinker' with boats and renovate with advice and 'a tot of rum.' The eldest of those experts was ninety-six. When one of the group died, the in-house joke said gently was, 'There'll be a boat going cheap!' *The camaraderie and routine meetings kept a sense of focus and new friendships were formed.*

- He was a farmer at one point with sheep high on a hillside, with prior long-term stays on a sheep farm in Southern Island, to learn from those successful in that role, before he bought his own stock.

And now? He carves wood, accepting challenges, new learning and often frustrated with his own limitations, but never more content.

What is to be learned here?

Not all of these projects were long term, but shaped the exit from one life to another, where rank and status matter not at all.

Yes, now I listen to that story from thirty-seven years ago when my dad asked himself the question of 'Who am I?'

Why? *Because like for so many people, the recent pandemic has meant changes in workplace or roles whilst, during the COVID-19 lockdowns, we were restricted to our homes, excluding one hour of exercise a day and a weekly doorstep clap for the NHS. However, if we are honest, we are not all clamouring back to what we did before.*

Ever increasing cost of living, imminent threat to peace overseas, but not that far away – and changes in our social culture have all played their part in this introspection.

Whether enforced or chosen, haven't we all in recent times had the silence and space, welcome or otherwise, to grapple with huge and often life changing questions?

For many, there is blended work practice, in part remote, whilst some aspects of the previous roles must remain in the office. Childcare – and pet care (let's face it, I had never heard of 'doggy day care', which is now a booming business) have become key considerations. The use of technology, no longer a novelty for a 'lockdown quiz', has continued to shape how we operate in the workplace. Indeed, we joked about newsreaders in previous generations possibly being only appropriately attired from desk upwards, but how many of us have held business meetings during the COVID-19 pandemic in a smart top, but also our slippers and even pyjama bottoms... *it can't just be me!*

When stepping into the unknown, taking that leap to life beyond lanyards, it naturally comes with deep reflection and a need to provide oneself with time and space to adapt, almost chrysalis-like, undertaking a metamorphosis into some new version of oneself, *ready to fly.* However, like that newly hatched butterfly with dampened wings, one finds oneself at times frail or vulnerable and needing a moment to re-establish or adjust to the new normal. *Our aim is to do this transition bravely, yes, but as safely as one can.*

Many of the case studies share my experience that, even if your initial choice of change doesn't work or evolves differently from the original plan, that isn't a reason to deter you. In fact, it can be the source of the of greatest learning of all.

Alan shares that, '*It is critical for anyone to have options in life and not to let others control your destiny at work or at home. To be in control, you need to make time to develop new skills, knowledge and interests which will help confidence and resourcefulness in the ability to move on and maybe take on a new job. There is little point in having a plan that is not well researched in terms of business ideas or more personal lifestyle objectives. Most individuals I advise did not do enough before the change.'*

Cate reflects on her life changing decision very clearly and with typical creative and positive assurance:

'If you aren't happy, 'get your brave on' and make the change.'

One size most certainly does not *nor should* not fit all, otherwise, the outcome for us all would be, by definition, identical. Natural skills and personality, personal circumstances and how dependent you are on others, or they on you, will all shape each person's trajectory. Nevertheless, the flight is still possible *and falling need not be an outcome at all. In fact, who knows what aerobatics are in store?*

However, the change can be in stages and still demonstrate courage, so how have these incredible people made their life beyond lanyards successful and fulfilling?

Iain recalls how easy it is, 'To *feel in awe of the experts around you but, reassuringly, whilst you will have much to learn, you will already have much experience and new ideas or ways of doing things that will be of great value in your new role.'*

Many of our case studies encourage us to listen to others and ask questions, but don't be deterred from challenging current practices – many things happen in a particular way, not because it's the best way, but because that's the way it's always been done. Sharon explains that:

'Change is always going to be scary. – Research as much as you can and ask others who have taken that route to give advice rather than take advice from people who have never been in that situation before. Try to focus on the positives and that will help to overshadow the negatives.'

Many of our case studies urge fellow travellers to talk to family and friends, ask for help *and accept the help offered!*

Alan and Jane celebrate the wonders of the internet, where tutorials can help us acquire new skills: I certainly admit to scanning, magpie-like, how others market their services and products, to shape my own new business. *Remember, comparison websites not only give information on pricing and quality of service, but customer reviews can highlight other people's pitfalls.* Simple practise opportunities can be through selling second-hand or unwanted items on an online platform and you soon get to know how to pitch, price and communicate in a way with minimal outlay, which is separate to your chosen area for the next role. Besides, you can make some money too!

Then there are blogs, audio access and LinkedIn which are full of people celebrating their own success! *Do they ever have an off day?*

What is abundantly clear, is that more and more people will embark on self-employment initiatives in years to come and more will establish themselves in roles yet to be dreamed of. Our entrepreneurial spirit will need to reignite, succinctly explained by Alan:

'The Organisation for Economic Cooperation and Development (OECD) predicts that by 2030, fifty per cent of the working population in its member countries will be freelance workers, the pandemic has accelerated this. That is a massive shift to self-employment and dynamic working practices. I recognise that for many, this will be a challenging decade and now is the time to build new skills and habits to prepare for an inevitable change in workplace culture.'

What are the key messages for a safe flight?

Practical advice on a 'to do' list: fasten those seatbelts:

- Know what you are looking for and be prepared to wait for it if necessary.
- Have a 'wish list' being specific, but also know what you are prepared to compromise on.
- Listen to your body and allow yourself to rest when needed.
- To try before you jump, if possible, maybe in a voluntary capacity.
- Use the experience of those around you.
- Do what you do for yourself and those that matter, *don't get sucked into trying to fulfil the expectations of others, especially if they are not significantly important to you.*
- When leaving an organisation, you don't need to sever all ties indefinitely, *but give yourself and your previous team time and space for dust to settle... (norming, forming, storming).*
- When an idea comes, explore all possibilities open to you!
- Choose options for what you need, not containing yourself with additional income, responsibility and stress as the only possible option.
- Trust your instincts, take the plunge – whatever happens, good or bad – it's an experience.
- Consider writing a journal to enable thought processes to emerge over time and be returned to for dismissing, or development. *Hence this book!*
- Remember to welcome the high days but acknowledge the low days too: they will pass.
- Accept a quiet day and welcome, rather than fear, the sound of silence and your own company.
- Say *yes please*, to opportunities *and yes please again to help when it is offered.*
- Pay off loans and mortgage before taking the leap, *if you have that choice.*
- Use professional mentors for specific purposes.

- Harvest good will from others, where you have previously given to them, – this time is for you!
- Consider coaching to ensure you look at the wider picture.
- Be financially disciplined.
- Know and abide by your own moral code to keep in sight what you want and what you will tolerate. *At times, choosing what feels right is essential.*
- Read as much as you can on business and personal development. There are thousands of publications out there, you must take the best parts and make them your own.
- If your career path is in the private sector, ALWAYS protect your pension provision whenever you change jobs.
- Be smart with your time, sixty-four per cent of your results come from just four per cent of your most effective time.
- Ensuring your wills are reviewed and updated as your circumstances change, and whatever your age: it is a thought-provoking, sobering but essential process.

Practical advice to avoid turbulence:
- Don't be restricted by low expectations of others: what you bring from your background is important and valuable.
- Don't allow yourself to get to burnout level before calling it quits.
- Don't go in blind!
- Don't let a lower wage impact on your choices (ideally), if you find something that works for you, interests you – and challenges you, go for it!
- Be careful whose advice you trust, true friends will have your best interests at heart.
- Be and stay focused on what you are trying to achieve.
- Always remember the rule of three: never have more than

three objectives about what you want to achieve and what you want to communicate.

- Don't over-rely on professional jargon or acronyms in your communication as often extended and specialist vocabulary doesn't communicate levels of understanding and benefits to others.
- Don't surround yourself just with those who will back you... a critical friend to ask challenging questions is invaluable.
- Take advice but cherry-pick what resonates for you and your circumstances.
- Make sure those around you are on board and share your vision. It will be a bumpy ride for them too.
- Get rid of the people who take you down, the negativity of those people is not helpful nor is it healthy.

Motivational encouragement from fellow travellers: 'reach for those stars!'

- Embrace both the excitement and trepidation of what the future holds, after all, it is our experiences that add spice to our lives!
- For some, faith in a religion or philosophy is hugely influential.
- Accept there remains much to learn and embrace that as an opportunity, *not something to be fearful of*.
- Be true to what you aspired for, so that life beyond lanyards *frees you* rather than imprisons you.
- Don't be afraid to dream, believe you can do it!
- Have fun!
- Figure out what you want to achieve and focus on it every day.
- The uncertainties associated with major life changes,

whether career or health, brings into sharper focus the necessity for clarity of legacy, particularly for your family.

- Life is always going to be challenging, we will only know if we can - if we try ... and who knows, maybe you will discover you are great at it!
- *Life is too short. Just get on with whatever you want to do, even if it just sitting around doing nothing.*
- Live life to the full. Don't leave it until tomorrow.
- The universe will provide the means for you to achieve what you want, even though it may not look like it.
- Recognise that everything happens for a reason – good or bad – and make it work for you: 'own it.'
- Richness is more than the bank account!
- Having a positive attitude, a willingness to learn and being open to all opportunities that present themselves is a winning combination!

You are not alone:
- In any life-changing events, it is important to have all parties on board, especially as children grow older; they want to feel that they are listened to and that their opinion matters.
- Opportunities will come your way that you could not have predicted. *All experience gained has value.*
- Be kind to others with your time and knowledge, *often what you give out, you will get back.*
- Friendships forged initially at work thought to be life-long may fade, due to a lack of common ground. However, others will remain, stronger by the distance from the previous workplace – and enriched by differences as well as shared interests and history.

So, what is to stop any of us from rethinking our priorities, needs against wants, aspiration versus accolades? Do we really need that lanyard to give us reason to feel successful and fulfilled?

Darren advises from the perspective of a professional who is often there in the last moments of someone's time on this earth: "*It's better to know it was not your path than think in later life, "What would have happened if?"*

Most powerfully, he reminds us not to leave this world with a gravestone saying, *"Returned unopened."*

Chapter 20

Boarding Passes at the Ready: Let's Fly!

Across professions, disciplines, culture, class and gender, we see people choosing a life beyond lanyards. Maybe this is a planned next step, long honed and dreamed of. Maybe it is something enforced upon us, unwelcome, unexpected or because of a life-changing health or family circumstances – all beyond our control. What is clear is that there is not one recipe for success for that leap, but the metaphorical skies are full of people who have launched themselves into the unknown, often unsure and usually with fears of falling.

Not all had a 'Martin Luther King-like dream' in international impact or clarity. However, they have all been brave, driven by a sense of needing to change. That could be through a faith-related epiphany, it could be through ill health, redundancy, or loss. The lucky ones have had the chance to choose and to plan life beyond lanyards. For that, their success is not just for themselves but here, shared for others to consider and perhaps support those preparing to leap into, what at times, can feel like a void.

What has become evident to me is how blessed I have been to have each of these incredible case studies as people who have been alongside me on my own personal journey.

I continue to be humbled by their openness and honesty.

In listening to others, especially these good folk share their advice, experience and feelings during their own transitions, I realise perhaps the last bit of learning for me, is to continue to be a collector: not of things that need dusting nor at risk of theft or damage; I pledge to continue to collect interesting people, and urge you as my reader to see who your motivators are, no doubt, they are hiding in plain sight.

Final considerations before setting your SATNAV on the next destination:

- Be prepared for a journey not always to be a motorway directed as a fast track to your next step: sometimes the meandering path embeds what is important and enriches with new experiences. Whilst unexpected, these influences can be enabling as well as inhibiting in equal measure. *Choose how to receive and respond to each with an open mind.*
- Consider your capacity for the amount of necessary time, level of risk and new learning against current capabilities and dependents.
- Plug any gaps you come across with new learning – *or by asking for help.*
- Rushing into a new adventure and cramming it with busy days without time to reflect simply defers the grieving process for what has been before and hinders useful progress intellectually as well as practically.

I have embraced the holidays, lunches, theatre trips and coffees without now feeling I was playing truant, *but the quieter days I dreaded are now equally valued, but took more time to embrace as part of my 'new normal,'*

This is in stark contrast to an earlier 'me', who returned to school as a head teacher from a local authority role, but with no formal training on how to lead such a primary school.

Certain parents who were incredibly welcoming, actually suggested, as I was sure to agree, that it was a shame I wasn't a man!

I remember sitting in that head's office, with imposter syndrome rampaging through my mind, my heart racing, to the point of feeling physically sick. What would I do all day, without a class to teach or a directive to determine my every action?

The answer came as I opened my professional head teacher diary for the first time, and wrote with considerable care, *'Open... post... slowly...'*

That calmed my nerves, filled a part of my day, and gave this particular professional person in uncharted waters, a chance to steady that ship and set course to successfully sail. Twenty-two years later, there is a new journey ahead, but this time with a scaffold of support and skills, some of which are only just becoming evident this very day.

Whatever your starting point, may your journey to a life beyond lanyards be enriched, happy and fulfilling.

Good luck!